Remember to Laugh

Writing My Way Around the World

Remember to Laugh

Writing My Way Around the World

Maggie Kilgore

ANOTHER *SMART BUSINESS* BOOK
FROM **THE WORK FACTORY**

A Division of Palari Publishing LLP
www.palaribooks.com

Remember to Laugh: Writing My Way Around the World
© 2006, By Maggie Kilgore

A WORK Factory Book
1113 West Main Street, Richmond, VA 23220
A division of Palari Publishing LLP
www.palaribooks.com

Inquiries should be addressed to: Permissions Department
Palari Publishing LLP, PO Box 9288 Richmond, VA 23227

Chapter 1 was originally written for the *Los Angeles Times* op-ed page - 1978. Reprinted with permission.

Helen Thomas story in Chapter 5 reprinted with the permission of Scribner, an imprint of Simon & Schuster Adult Publishing Group, from THANKS FOR THE MEMORIES, MR PRESIDENT: WIT AND WISDOM FROM THE FRONT ROW AT THE WHITE HOUSE by Helen Thomas. Copyright © 2002 by Helen Thomas.

Library of Congress Cataloging-in-Publication Data

Kilgore, Maggie, 1935-
  Remember to laugh : writing my way around the world / Maggie Kilgore.
      p. cm.
  Includes index.
  ISBN-13: 978-1-928662-37-2 (hardcover)
  ISBN-10: 1-928662-37-4 (hardcover)
  ISBN-13: 978-1-928662-38-9 (pbk.)
  ISBN-10: 1-928662-38-2 (pbk.)
  1. Kilgore, Maggie, 1935- 2. Women journalists--United States--Biography. 3. Journalists--United States--Biography. I. Title.
  PN4874.K535A3 2006
  070.92--dc22

                                                                2006007255

Printed in the United States of America
10 9 8 7 6 5 4 3 2 1

Editor: Dave Smitherman
Cover design: Ted Randler

Photos are from author's personal collection unless otherwise indicated.

To Jason Kilgore Rice,
my nephew who left the party of life too soon,
and to the other members of my family.

TABLE OF CONTENTS

ACKNOWLEDGEMENTS

It seems that everyone has a book in mind or one in the computer, partially written. During the course of writing this book, I heard from total strangers who said they heard that I had a literary agent and a publisher—and would I mind sharing their names?

Then they launched into their proposal on the telephone, and I was a captive audience for too many minutes. The most amazing—if you can call it that—question I received was from a friend's ex-husband who said he had a cousin who was prepared to write "the funny side of the Holocaust" and did I think it would sell? I was so floored by the question that I referred him to the Museum of Tolerance in Beverly Hills for an answer.

Let them deal with it.

No one can write a book without help and I am no exception. At the risk of sounding like a Hollywood awards show, I want to pay tribute to my literary agent, lawyer and friend Diane S. Nine in Washington who has helped me every step of the way. The group at Palari Publishers in Richmond—David Smitherman and Ted Randler—have given me professional and efficient support and marvelous encouragement. My longtime friend, Daniel Rapoport and my cousin Victor Dix, both retired publishers, contributed advice and added stories to the manuscript along with the indefatigable Helen Thomas, of course.

Bob and Catherine Kaylor and Barbara and Dennis Cook helped me recall the turbulent Vietnam years. Gar and Barbara Kaganowich, John and Susie Hall, Isabelle and Stan

Hall, Louise Hutchinson, and Al Spivak weighed-in with tales from the Ohio, New Jersey and Washington years. My good and loyal pals, Betsy Balsley and Rob Wood, gave me editing support on the Los Angeles sections and kept me on target. Chris and Bernie Roswig gave me valuable public relations input in between our golf games. Carol Scott reminded me of our various escapades in the later Asian years and the Schwarzes' and Don Thompson confirmed the German tales.

I am very indebted to all of them for the time and effort they took to help me and the memories they shared or helped me recall. I think it was fun for them, too. It also has helped to have two trunks of old news clippings dating back to Columbus/UPI days which helped me remember the circumstances of many events. Sometimes being a 'pack rat' isn't all bad. My late mother also kept my letters to her from my travels which filled some major gaps, especially during the Vietnam War period. If you remember the incidents differently, I look forward to reading your book.

Finally, I want to thank my sister and brother-in-law, Martha and Norman Rice, and my brother Alfred Hall who are always there when I need them to listen, to love, and to laugh.

I hope you enjoyed the book as much as I enjoyed writing it.

Maggie Kilgore
Santa Monica, CA

FOREWORD

Journalist Maggie Kilgore has written a marvelous memoir about her years working for newspapers and the wire service, United Press International.

She covered major stories in Washington and went on to become a war correspondent in Vietnam. She has had a long and successful career which she tells about with great humor.

I admit to being prejudiced in her favor because we have been friends and colleagues for nearly half a century, in good times and bad. As you will read in the book, we have had many adventures as women journalists in a profession once dominated by men. We have paid our dues to journalism while having some fun along the way.

I entered journalism during World War II when men were being called to war literally if they could breathe. Maggie came along in the next wave of women in the 1960s that benefited from our progress, and she continued to work to advance women in the media.

We have lived through the changes that have come to our profession, not all of them good, but we have been participants in "giving back" to a noble cause, freedom of the press. Our years with UPI and beyond were active, productive and important. UPI is like a big fraternity. No matter where we go in the world—in Africa, Asia or the 50 states—chances are we will meet someone who worked for the old wire service who wants to share the experience.

I always say to Maggie *mi casa, su casa* and she does the same. Although she lives in California and I still live in

Washington, we meet on both coasts frequently to share confidences, gossip and laugh. That's what friends do. There has never been rivalry between us and we are always in touch. She's a good cook, too. Her superb book, *Remember to Laugh: Writing My Way Around the World,* will go a long way in giving readers a lift and respite from the grim news we deal with daily. I hope you enjoy it because it's a different perspective on a couple of working girls' lives.

Helen Thomas, Columnist
Hearst Newspapers, Washington, D.C.

INTRODUCTION

U nlike other writers with a personal story to tell, I am not a victim of abuse, nor did I have a weird grandfather or a strange uncle. My parents didn't beat me.

In fact, my family wasn't even poor or downtrodden. I was given a good education with help, love, luck, and some sadness along the way. My mother's large family is in the newspaper, radio/TV business in Ohio. They certainly influenced my decision to go into journalism which fortunately has meant travel and adventure over much of the world.

People say to me "Oh, you meet such interesting people in journalism." Yes, other reporters and editors. Like cops, we are a clannish breed. We would rather talk to each other than to outsiders. This, of course, leads to criticism of "pack journalism," but for me it also has meant lifelong friendships with a very loyal bunch of fun-loving men and women.

I decided to write this book to tell humorous stories about my experiences and those of my friends who have worked overseas, in Washington, and elsewhere in newspapers, teaching, entertainment and public relations over a 40-year period. To set the stage, I also have included several family stories to tell my personal history.

I was a foreign correspondent in Vietnam for 21 months (and returned later), a state government and Washington reporter, a manager for the casino industry, and an educator in the U.S. and overseas in Third World countries. I've flown with the Blue Angels, landed on an aircraft carrier, and spent a long afternoon on the Goodyear blimp.

Yes, I have encountered discrimination along the way as a woman in the once male-dominated journalism profession, but many men have helped me to succeed.

I've always worked because that's what I like to do. As Willie Sutton said about robbing banks, that's where the money is. Or, as the late Duchess of Windsor commented, "You can't be too rich or too thin." Right. Or have too many friends, male and female.

One of my early mentors, Maureen McKernan Ross of the Macy newspaper chain in Westchester County, New York, remarked when I was young and insecure, "Well, at least you aren't too pretty. You'll be able to make it on your talent instead of just your good looks." Talk about a left-handed compliment.

This book is not a treatise on world peace, although I certainly support it. I want to amuse and interest you, not bore you. So, let's get started.

Up, up and away!

1

CALIFORNIA
The Blue Skies

Eat your heart out, Red Baron. I was Wonder Woman. I was Amelia Earhart. I was Lois Lane, flying with Superman, my long chiffon scarf trailing behind me for glamour and luck. Then the pilot announced we were going into a barrel roll and I snapped out of my reverie. As the original white-knuckle flier, I was 5,000 feet and climbing over Newport Beach, California and in grave danger of becoming terminally airsick.

I held on tight and my stomach rolled with it. There was sky above us. Then sky below us. The horizon had disappeared. I felt as though I had just been recruited out of Central Casting for *The High and the Mighty*.

The Navy pilot pulled on the stick of the two-passenger turbo-prop warplane and we leveled off, floating through the clouds at 11,000 feet. "And now we're going to do the four-point hesitation roll," he said. I clenched my teeth as the Blue Angel began to dive.

It was no experience for the fainthearted. When I arrived at the Marine Corps Air Station at El Toro to begin the flight, two TV newsmen had already flown and were congratulating themselves on being so brave.

Navy and Marine pilots belonging to the Blue Angels Flight Demonstration Squadron are a kind of military elite, aerial tricksters who lure young men and women into the military.

One of the newsmen proudly announced he hadn't been air-sick, which seemed to transfer the burden of survival to me. The last passenger shed his khaki jumpsuit, allegedly fireproof, and handed it over. I put it on and with the aid of a mechanic climbed up the ladder to the cockpit of the Skyhawk II. I hoped that the plane really hadn't been built by the lowest bidder.

I remembered the flight crew's advice. If you allow your eyes to focus on the horizon or on a fixed object in the plane, you probably won't become disoriented. A good tip, if I could just summon the courage to open my eyes.

I took some comfort that the parachute was built into the seat —or so they promised me. The pilot, a short, thin man who brought to mind Jockey Willie Shoemaker and not Steve Canyon, the comic book hero, climbed up front joking about this being his first flight.

"How do you run this darn thing," he asked the mechanic.

Maybe I wasn't Amelia Earhart taxiing down the runway, but I had been through some pretty hairy incidences during my two years as a foreign correspondent in Vietnam, including an escape from a chopper fire in the Delta and a landing and catapult off an aircraft by jet in the Gulf of Tonkin. So why was there a sinking feeling in the pit of my stomach?

It flashed through my mind that the Blue Angels have suffered crashes and fatalities, mostly at air shows, in past years. They don't fly in formation with civilians because of the danger. It doesn't pay to be two well-informed. Onward and upward.

"Can I call you *Maggie* instead of Margaret?" The pilot asked as the vertical lift plane came quickly off the pavement. Since my life was literally in his hands, I felt we should be as friendly as a tandem aircraft will allow. I nodded in the direction of his rearview mirror.

"We are now off the runway and ready for takeoff," he said,

talking to the tower and to me. I had been told we would take off straight up, but it was like sitting in a dentist's chair waiting for the drill to strike a nerve.

We tilted upward in what is known in the trade as a low-transit high-performance climb, like a rocket. My body strained involuntarily against the seat belt and shoulder straps, like a convict getting the juice in an electric chair.

Confidentially, I did wonder what I was doing there and thought fleetingly of my elderly mother in upstate New York and my family, who undoubtedly would miss me. I gritted my teeth and leaned my head, encased in a black helmet, against a brace. I was strapped in so securely I could scarcely breathe. Or perhaps the thrust took my breath away. It was difficult to tell.

Within seconds, the pilot pulled on the stick and we leveled off over the Pacific Ocean. "We're now doing 450 miles an hour," he announced, adding "Why don't you pull that lever by your left hand and loosen the seat slightly, so you'll be more comfortable?" Comfortable? He had to be kidding.

I was afraid anything I touched would eject me into the wild blue yonder, but I did as I was told and was able to reach another white button which gave us two-way communication. I always feel better when I can talk to someone.

The pilot told me had been a Blue Angel for a year and he had 2,500 hours of flying time on his record. To qualify for the team, a pilot must have accrued a minimum of 1,200 hours of flying time and be an active duty Navy or Marine Corps tactical jet pilot. The average age of the pilots is 33. A friend who disapproved of my caper had gratuitously pointed out that I was a day or two older than that.

The clouds pushed around the windows like smoke and the sun made the cabin uncomfortably warm. Or maybe that was my blood boiling over. Below us, the clouds blotted out the land and we saw little of the blue of the Pacific as we cruised to a radio point off Santa Catalina Island, about 20 miles from the mainland.

Someone told me to be sure and do a figure 8. "Gee, you're brave," the pilot joked. "Are you sure you want to do it?"

"Sure," I replied. What did I know?

We began a full Cuban-8 roll, which consists of flying upside down, dipping down and then righting the plane. And next, to complete the figure 8, flying forward, plunging downward and circling upward again. It was like riding Montezooma's Revenge at Knott's Berry Farm amusement park, only worse.

We headed back to the base then, and other aircraft were instructed to wait until we landed. Good thing, too, with all of those tax dollars riding with us. The mechanic who had strapped me in 40 minutes before climbed up the ladder to the cockpit to unstrap me. He seemed genuinely relieved that I hadn't fainted or vomited, or otherwise messed up his cockpit.

Indeed. Wonder Woman wouldn't have fainted, would she? Or Amelia. Or Lois.

With a smart salute to the pilot and crew, I squared my shoulders and swaggered—some might say lurched—away. My chiffon scarf casually trailed behind me.

Snoopy would have been proud.

My parents, Donna and Alfred Kilgore,
with me at age three months in the 1930s.

2

OHIO
Journalist or Flight Attendant?

W hen I was born, they nicknamed me "Happy." My mother had a black nurse named May-May who said the name fit because I was such a happy baby. Evidently she said that because I didn't have colic. I've always said that I could tell which stage of my life someone knew me by what they call me—if it's complimentary.

If they knew me before I was 22, they still call me Happy or Hap. In my family, few of us were called by our rightful names.

After I finished college, became a journalist and went to work for United Press International, I became "Maggie." The late Bernie Buttler, day editor at UPI in Columbus, Ohio in 1957, said Maggie was a good name for a girl reporter. It would sound tough and aggressive, he said, and look good in a byline. The name stuck although I never used it in a byline...until I wrote this book.

I am formally named after two of my aunts, Margaret and Adelaide.

A Depression-era baby of the '30s, I was the oldest and first of three daughters born to Alfred David and Donna Voorhees Kilgore, then living in Elyria, Ohio, a Cleveland suburb. I actually was born at a hospital in Ravenna, Ohio, because that's where my mother's doctor practiced. (One time when I was clearing Customs in Calcutta, India, the agent smiled when he saw Ravenna, Ohio on my passport/visa papers. "I was an exchange student at Kent State, 10 miles away," he said, waving me on.)

My parents waited six years after their marriage to have me because of uncertain economic times. However, I once asked mother if they had suffered during the Great Depression as so many people did.

"No," she replied. "We didn't have enough real money to suffer. We both had jobs and we did all right." Dad had a mid-level executive position with General Motors Acceptance Corporation in Cleveland, Akron and Canton, Ohio. We moved several times between those three cities when I was under the age of eight.

Mother worked at "the charities" (welfare department) in Cleveland until she became so emotionally upset over the plight of the poor and the hard times that she quit the job.

Three years after I was born, my parents had another daughter, Donna Jane, who died of a heart defect within 24 hours. She is buried in Wooster, Ohio, in the family plot.

In 1939, my sister, Mary Martha, was born, pretty and healthy. We are all very close as a family, but it's a situation that needs constant care, just like a good marriage. Healthy relationships don't just happen. They have to be nurtured.

Mother was the youngest of five children, evidently a menopause baby, because her closest sister, Adelaide, was nine years older. The oldest sister, Edna, married Emmet Dix, owner of the newspaper, radio and television chain headquartered in Wooster.

Mother had a colorful career as a dramatic actress before she married dad, unusual for a young woman in the 1920s—long before women's liberation—but about the time of women's suffrage.

Encouraged by the family when she showed early talent, Mother studied at the Lyceum Arts Conservatory in Chicago while living in Oak Park, Il. with her older brother, Martin, a dentist and his wife, Margaret (Madge).

Mother wasn't a great beauty, but she was a tall, thin brunette with a deep, cultured voice, a sense of humor, and a keen understanding and tolerance of others. She was christened "Effie Page," but changed her name to Donna when her brother renamed her after his favorite cigar, LaDonna.

In the early part of the 20th century, there were traveling theater companies, generically called Chautauqua, that traveled from town to town and abroad, bringing performances, lectures, and religion to the farmers and locals in the hinterland. Mother joined one of the troupes, Ellison and White, for nearly a decade as an actress and also worked as an advance person for upcoming shows, traveling to small towns in the West and Midwest. An avid horsewoman, she perfected her riding skills in the mountains of the West.

She also parlayed her acting success into overseas travel by ship to such far-off locales as Australia, Tahiti, Fiji, and other South Pacific points. I have a small wooden canoe she bought as a souvenir which says "Fiji-1925."

It was an experience she never forgot and she regaled us with her adventures at the dinner table when we were teenagers, broadening our horizons. The women in my family have always been independent achievers and the men in their lives supported them in many ways.

Mother met my father through mutual friends soon after she returned to Wooster from her theatrical years. Her sister, Adelaide, divorced from a second marriage, was working as a secretary, raising my cousin John alone, and trying to care for their elderly widowed mother, my grandmother Emma (nicknamed Bondie) in Wooster. For a time the two sisters operated a dance studio in Wooster, which many older residents mentioned to me when I worked on the newspaper. Bondie, an active suffragette, died before I was born.

In the-apple-doesn't-fall-far-from-the-tree mode, my sister, my second cousin Ellen, and my sister's youngest child Caitlin have all tried their hand at show business only to realize what a hard life it is to catch a break, and eventually switched careers.

Dad was born in Anderson, Indiana, in an area where many Protestant Scotch Irish settled when they made the migration from northern Ireland in the 1800s. He had an older sister, Mary.

Their mother, Minnie May, had an unhappy childhood with older parents. She left home at 18 to marry a farmer named Kilgore, father of Alfred and Mary, but he died when the children were young.

She subsequently married an Indiana state senator and oil wild-catter named Lewis V. Ulrey. Minnie, known as Nicky to the family, thought she had a happy and durable marriage the second time around. Lew was good to dad and Mary, so much so that dad used his stepfather's name, Ulrey, until he reached adulthood and took back the name Kilgore. Dad was a graduate of Kenyon College in Gambier, Ohio, with tuition paid by Ulrey.

However, Lew and Minnie apparently weren't as happy as she thought. He was away from home for long periods of time on oil exploration expeditions in the Southwest and Mexico. She said he told her before he left on his last trip that he would be home as soon as one of his oil wells started producing. He never returned. No letters, no messages. Nothing.

The family hired private investigators to search for Ulrey, and Minnie visited Mexico, but communications in the early part of the 20th century were inadequate, and a person who didn't want to be found could disappear unhindered. They didn't know if he was dead or alive.

Ulrey was missing for more than seven years. Minnie obtained a divorce on grounds of abandonment, but she never forgot Lew and always thought he would come back to her if he was physically able—or had struck oil. His disappearance left her totally dependent on her two grown children. She shuttled back and forth between their homes in Ohio and New York for the rest of her life.

I asked mother once if it was difficult having her mother-in-law underfoot so much. "That's what families did," she said simply. "They took care of each other."

An attractive, proud woman with a good figure, even in her later years, Minnie (Nicky) was much adored by her four grandchildren. She spent her afternoons in bed listening to radio soap operas and we considered it a treat if she let us snuggle down with her to hear *Stella Dallas* or *Mary Noble, Backstage Wife*. She had an interest in the occult and never tired of telling us ghost stories and weird happenings. She kept a tin chamber pot under her bed which she let us use (more interesting than a toilet) and slept with a silver knife stuck in her locked bedroom door jamb because "one couldn't be too careful at night."

One time she decided that my dad should wear a men's girdle to mask his pot belly and went to a department store in Akron to find it. She mistakenly took me with her and I caused such a crying tantrum in the store when I thought she was going to make my dad wear a girdle like mother did that she finally abandoned the idea. Dad thought the whole idea was hilarious, but he didn't fund the girdle project either.

Nicky, whose maiden name was "Hoover," told us she was a distant cousin of President Herbert Hoover, the nation's 31st president. She sent him a congratulatory telegram when he was elected and received a pro forma reply from the White House. Her grandson, Alfred, and his son both carry Hoover as their middle names, but like Ulrey's return, the Hoover relationship may be another fantasy.

Dad and Aunt Mary were both of the opinion that Lew was an

honorable man, but that Nicky's nagging and constant demands probably drove him away. This theory was borne out some 20 years later after Dad and Mary had died and Nicky was an invalid. One day in the 1940s, publisher Emmet Dix was thumbing through a copy of an old *Saturday Evening Post* when he came upon a photo of a congressional hearing on oil exploration. Prominently featured were several oil drilling executives including "Lewis V. Ulrey of Indiana, a former state senator."

Emmet showed the picture to my widowed mother. Mother, swearing me to secrecy, showed me the picture before the magazine was discarded. Nicky was living with us in Wooster at the time, but her health was so frail that Emmet and mother never told her. Nicky died never knowing that Lew was alive and well, apparently deliberate in his actions. I've always wished I could have met him and asked him why, but I was still a child and some things in families are better left unsaid or undiscovered.

My family's tangled relationships played a key role in exposing me to the world of journalism and travel. In fact, one of mother's beaus during the Chautauqua days was the famous newspaper and radio columnist Drew Pearson who went on to write *The Washington Merry-Go-Round* with his partner, Robert S. Allen and later Jack Anderson. Pearson became a lifelong friend of our family, visiting mother and father in Ohio often. He and his late wife, Luvie, entertained me in their Georgetown home when I visited Washington on my high school class trip. After I became a Washington reporter and President of the Women's National Press Club, he wrote Mother a gracious letter saying how proud he was of me and his long friendship with our family.

In his book *Reporting from Washington* (Oxford University Press 2005), congressional historian Donald A. Ritchie said that Pearson had the reputation among his peers for being "the best rat-catching reporter in town."

Ritchie also notes that "after a youth spent organizing parades to advertise Chautauqua meetings, Andrew Russell Pearson, a Quaker, retained the flair of a carnival huckster. In the 1920s, he had set out as a vagabond journalist traveling around the world and paying his way through lectures and freelance reporting."

I have a letter from Pearson—who always was controversial and proud of it—dated January 30, 1945 during Franklin D. Roosevelt's final term in office, commenting on Jesse Jones, head of the Reconstruction Finance Corp. at the end of World War II.

> *I tried to say something about Jesse Jones on the air, but my radio people didn't like it and made me cut part of it out. You see, Jesse Jones owns one of the radio stations over which I broadcast.*
>
> *When you grow up, you will understand better the power of some people who have a lot of money and own radio stations.*

Pearson's personally typewritten letter was in reply to a thank-you note I had written him for a pin in the shape of a little bronze horse which I still have. I was 10 at the time. Thanks to cousin Raymond Dix, who succeeded his father as publisher, I worked on the *Wooster Daily Record* during college summers correcting page proofs and being allowed to cover the county courthouse, an experience which made me think I knew everything there was to know about reporting when I returned to college. In fact, I did know as much as many of the college journalism professors who went straight to academia and never worked on publications or on radio. Television was still in its infancy.

The Dixes always played a prominent role in our branch of the family. The operation was in the hands of the fourth and fifth gen-

eration of Dixes in 2006, one of the few family-owned and operated media conglomerates left in America. There is no question
that I was influenced as a child to enter journalism by listening to
Emmet's stories of covering the news and mother's talk of her
global travels, both making me aware of the world outside Ohio. I
also wanted to be an airline flight attendant, but at 5'9" I was considered too tall.

Julie Photography

At Stephens College, 1954.

3

FLORIDA & NEW YORK
Multiple Job Offers

Mother married her brother-in-law. My first cousins became my stepbrothers. Our lives changed completely, but I'm getting ahead of my story.

Dad, a big, tall, jolly man with a hearty laugh, a love of fishing, reading, cussing, and beer was born a "blue baby" with insufficient oxygen who was said to be so small that he fit into a quart cup at birth. (Mother used to say it was a tea cup, but she exaggerated.)

The doctor is said to have looked at him, laid him aside as stillborn, and then changed his mind when the infant started to yell. Dad and his sister Mary apparently had healthy childhoods, but the medical profession didn't know as much about heart disease and birth defects as they do now, and future problems weren't detected. Dad died of coronary heart disease at 44; Mary had a fatal cerebral hemorrhage while working in her garden a year later.

Since there often is humor, even in tragedy, the "sandwich crisis" seemed to dominate Dad's funeral at Billows Funeral Home in Akron. Mother had a 300-pound-plus housekeeper named Louise who had a boyfriend, Clarence, who was a little person. In the middle of the funeral service when we were all seated, Louise, not the brightest bulb on the tree, waddled up to mother, tapped her on the shoulder and demanded "Clarence's sandwiches." Looking blank at the intrusion, Mother told Louise in effect to sit down and shut up. It seems that Clarence had left his job to attend the service, missed lunch, and Louise was trying to accommodate him like a good girlfriend would. Her timing was terrible.

The family had a reception for the mourners after the service at a restaurant near the funeral home. When we walked in, Louise was standing at the sandwich and cake table filling a large paper grocery sack with lunch for Clarence. Mother just grinned and passed the phrase "family, hold back" so our guests could be fed. She should have fired Louise, but she didn't. The story became part of the family folklore.

As the oldest daughter, I adored my father and I could do no wrong in his eyes. He taught me to fish with him and to read books like *Tom Sawyer* and *Huckleberry Finn* when other children my age were still reading nursery rhymes. He and Mother were happily married for 16 years, but in the final years I think he knew he wasn't going to live to see his daughters grow up. My sister Martha was so young when Dad died that she barely remembers him, which is unfortunate because he loved to hold her as a baby, talking and singing bar-room ballads to her like *Abdul the Bul Bul Emir* and *The Lady in Red*.

After he suffered his first heart attack (there were several), he took a leave from GMAC and we went to Miami Beach for three months to live at Emmet Dix's beach house. Those were the World War II years. Travel was difficult, but we managed to secure a stateroom. There were four of us traveling by train from Akron to Washington to Florida, sharing space with soldiers who were going south to training bases or to join the war.

The time we spent in Florida was fun. I was enrolled in the third grade in a Southern-style pink stucco school with the rooms opening onto a long double-deck verandah overlooking Biscayne Bay. I felt very grown up taking a public bus to school every day, clutching my round-trip 50-cent ticket.

The beach house had a large plate glass window in the living room which we were required by the military to cover every night with heavy black curtains to hide the light from the house. There were constant reports on radio and in the newspapers of German submarines and planes offshore—or the threat of them—although I'm not aware that Miami was ever bombed.

Coastguardsmen patrolled the beach every night, young men who befriended Dad and would surreptitiously stop by the house for a rest and a beer during the long work shift. They were a long way from the war zone, but they were bored, homesick and anxious to chat with civilians. I learned my multiplication tables by practicing in front of these young sailors and my parents, in the long evenings we spent together in the darkened living room.

Emmet, not a man to have his routine interrupted, took an arm chair and his newspaper to a second floor walk-in closet with a single hanging lightbulb, closed and taped the door so that no light could escape, and spent his evenings comfortably reading the newspaper. I wondered why he didn't suffocate in the heat.

One time, Dad and Mother took a war surplus rubber boat we had, climbed in with no oars, and began floating in the Atlantic on a sandbar in front of the house. As I think about it, I can't believe my intelligent parents were so stupid. Neither one of them knew how to swim, dad was a heart patient, and the tide was up with an offshore breeze.

They were talking and floating and ignoring the drift. Suddenly, they were far out in the water, heading for the shipping lanes, and unable to paddle back to shore. My cousin John McCulloch and his fiancée Helen, both young and in great physical shape, were standing on the patio watching them, unaware that there might be trouble. Suddenly, they saw my parents both signaling frantically.

John and Helen dove into the tide and kept on swimming until they reached the boat. Dad and Mother grabbed onto the swimmers' feet and slowly made their way back to shore. There was, of course, great speculation among us where they would have floated if help hadn't arrived, or the embarrassment if the U. S. Coast Guard had to be summoned. My sister and I were soon enrolled in swimming lessons.

Our next-door neighbor on Atlantic Way was the fourth-ranked world heavyweight boxer Tom Heeney, known as "The Hard Rock from Down Under" because of his New Zealand background. He had distinguished himself on July 26, 1928 when he fought for the world heavyweight championship at Yankee Stadium in New York against the skilled Gene Tunney.

The 15-round fight was called in the 11th round with Heeney losing, but he remains the only New Zealand-born challenger for the title. He was inducted into the New Zealand Sports Hall of Fame in 1996.

Heeney and his American wife Marion were a nice couple and visited back and forth with my parents during our time there. After 69 professional bouts, Heeney was punch-drunk and had difficulty completing sentences, but he was friendly and liked to laugh. He owned a restaurant in Miami and fished with author Ernest Hemingway. The couple had no children, but Marion, who was alone during the day and worked at the restaurant at night, spent time teaching me to swim. She died in 1980 and Tom passed away in 1984. His record was 32 wins, 22 losses, and 10 draws.

After Dad's death, life was difficult. He didn't live long enough to accumulate many financial assets and Mother, as a former actress, had few jobs skills to offer. Also, there was a war on. We stayed in our rented house in Akron for about a year, until we moved to Wooster to be near mother's family. The final catastrophe in Akron occurred when our beloved dog, Dick, a Pointer, was hit by a truck when he slipped his leash and ran into traffic. I discovered his body in the neighbor's yard as I came home from school on my birthday. It was time to move on.

Mother started taking classes at the College of Wooster, but it was slow going and money was tight. It was during that period that she instilled in sister Martha and me the need for a college education with practical skills included. Martha became a college instructor and I became a journalist, reassured that we could make a living no matter what happened in life.

Soon after Aunt Mary died, we took the train to Westfield, New York, for a month to help her husband, Harold Hall (Hal) and his two sons, Jim and Al, recover from the loss of their wife and mother. When the month was up we were still there, Hal and Mother fell in love and married about a year later. They were married for 18 years until his death in the 1960s.

If it sounds simple, it wasn't. There was considerable turmoil as the two families blended, and I was the cause of some of the dissension, but not all of it. Hal and Jim and Al weren't used to having so many females around and they missed Mary. I refused to accept Hal as my stepfather because I still wanted my dad to be there and I was spoiled as the first-born daughter. We weren't a dysfunctional family, but we had our bad moments. Blame it on adolescent angst.

It should have been an easier transition for me because I had visited Westfield many times as a niece and cousin, but to realize we were going to be there "forever" made me feel hurt and resentful at the age of 12. Also, I learned of their impending marriage from my friend Mags who said, "It's all over town that Hal and Donna are going to get married." I denied it until I confronted Mother, who confirmed it, which made me even more resentful. I thought "Mother and I were buddies after Dad's death, and shared confidences like the Lew Ulrey episode. As you can see, I was in heavy denial of life as it was.

The situation was exacerbated by my sociology teacher at school, Mr. Ramm, who cited mother-marrying-her-brother-in-law as some freakish happening comparing us to the Jukes-Kallikak clan.

(Jukes-Kallikak was the fictitious name of an actual family who were the focus of a sociological study: one branch were feeble-minded degenerates while another branch with descendants of normal intelligence were mostly successful. I was never sure which branch he thought we belonged to.)

When other kids started to tease me, I asked Ramm to stop mentioning our family in such terms, but he ignored me. I didn't need him to tell me and my classmates that I couldn't marry my stepbrothers because we were blood relatives and our children might be idiots. Who wanted to marry them anyway? Or they, us? We were barely speaking to each other most of the time.

In later years when we were all close again, Hal and Mother liked to joke that I actually brought them together because of my opposition to an elderly lawyer in Wooster who mother had started dating before we went to Westfield. No one was going to replace my daddy, and I'm sure the lawyer had no intention of doing so, but one couldn't be sure.

Hal, a lifelong Republican who had attended the University of Michigan with Thomas E. Dewey, was devastated in 1948 when Harry S. Truman upset Dewey for president.

"There goes the republic!" Hal intoned at the lunch table that day, looking grim.

Westfield is a picture postcard farming village of less than 5,000 residents in western New York between Erie, PA and Buffalo, NY. It is in the heart of Concord grape country, two miles from Lake Erie and the last stop on the New York State Thruway going West. Three generations of Halls managed Grower's Cooperative Grape Juice Co. and the family was prominent in the community. It was a good place to grow up even if the winters were difficult.

Because of its proximity to one of the Great Lakes, Iroquois Indian tribes or their derivatives originally roamed the area. In the early 1900s and beyond, Westfield was a main stop on the New York Central Railroad with guests alighting from New York and Chicago to travel by carriage 10 miles to visit the Chautauqua Institution cultural arts center. The railroad and the Erie Canal, near Buffalo, had been built by Italian, Sicilian, and Polish immigrants who remained to settle the area. They found work in the steel mills of Buffalo, and fertile land for growing grapes, tomatoes, apples, cherries, and other varieties of fruits and vegetables. Processing plants like Welch Grape Juice Co. and Growers were established to bottle and can the crops for wholesale shipment around the country.

The immigrants prospered, many of their children went to college and became successful citizens. Unfortunately, like many small towns, the second and third generation offspring who had bettered themselves moved to larger towns and cities to make a living because little towns like Westfield couldn't support them.

The passenger train service stopped as air travel advanced. The thruway bypassed the town, hurting tourism and the many antique shops there. Shoppers and diners went to Erie or Buffalo for entertainment. Western New York went into an economic slump in the 1950s, from which it has never really recovered.

For those of us who grew up there, we like to go back to Westfield because it rarely changes in appearance and it always seems like home.

In recent years, however, many of the young people who left to seek their fortunes have returned to the area to retire and young people with families have moved there to escape the crime and high prices of a city. They have purchased the large old homes owned by parents and grandparents and renovated them for their present needs. It is a trend that has helped rejuvenate many areas of the country.

The Presbyterian and Episcopal churches, with their tall spires, are the main features of the village green in the center of town along with an old mansion maintained as a museum. Westfield resembles a New England community except it isn't that far east.

When Mary was still alive, I visited the old Victorian house on Elm Street where they lived while I was still "the niece from Ohio." The house had a marvelous tower room at the top with wide floorboards and open knotholes so it was possible to see two floors down into the parlor. One day, Mary was entertaining the preacher in the parlor when Jim, Al and I, all under the age of 8, got into a pissing contest (literally) up in the tower. As the urine rained down into the parlor, Mary, suspecting the cause, wiped her eyes and weakly blamed it on a leaking water pipe in the ceiling. She was not amused, but the boys and I had a wonderful time. Jim, who was oldest, won.

About the same time, Jim and Al went off to Camp in the Woods, a YMCA camp on nearby Bear Lake, for two weeks. I was envious and wanted to go, too, so Hal paid to send me for a week to sleep in a tent, practice swimming and boating, and fight mosquitoes. It made me appreciate the comfort of luxurious spas as an adult.

By the time Mother, Martha and I appeared on the scene, the family had moved to Hal's home which he had inherited from his parents, a much larger place with riding horses and a barn where we used to have square dances as teenagers. It was later moved to the back of the property, converted to a duplex and owned by brother Al and me as rental property until we sold it.

Across the street from the main house was a large, spooky mansion inhabited by a woman named Anna Christina and her husband whom she called "The Colonel." The Colonel was a mysterious man who came and went for long periods of time. Hal said he was a bookie at the New York racetracks. The Colonel, described by Anna Christina as a naturalist, let his grass grow so high that residents in this neighborhood of well-tended, landscaped lawns complained. His solution was to buy a herd of goats to graze in the front yard and eat nearly anything. He also cut down some nice old trees, probably for firewood.

Anna Christina was forced to heat the house by fireplaces and for a time she burned candles to light the rooms because The Colonel didn't believe in electricity—or couldn't pay the bill. For her part, Anna, who claimed to be a former opera singer from Baltimore, would entertain us by singing and playing arias on the piano on warm summer nights when her windows were open.

Walking down the street she wore large theatrical hats with stuffed birds on top, long before such things were banned by endangered species laws. Their past was murky, but she was a kind, dignified woman who didn't seem to mind the noise we teens made across the street.

In obviously reduced circumstances, she put up a huge metal sign in the front yard which said "Spiritualist Readings. Anna Christina." The sign was great target practice with hunting rifles on Halloween for my brothers and their pals. Her outhouse also mysteriously disappeared one year, found by the police in the center of town under Westfield's only stoplight. The sheriff returned it to its rightful place behind her house and befriended her. His official car was often parked in the driveway when The Colonel was gone, leading to unverified romance speculation.

When she died, she left mother some nice antique jewelry in

her Will with a note saying that my family were the only one in town who had treated her with respect over the years. She apparently chose to overlook the Halloween incidents.

I acquired my first bra, my first formal gown (yellow chiffon), and my first kiss at the Christmas Charity Ball. My longtime friend Martha was dating Bill, son of a local antique dealer, and I dated Jack, a member of the Welch Grape Juice family, the "kiss perp." Both Bill and Jack went on to have successful careers, but they married others. Jane, Martha, Maxine, Marie, and Mags made up our group of teenagers along with a few others. We liked to think we ran the high school social life of the '50s, for better or worse.

One time a girl who wanted to be in our clique asked Mags how to do it. Mags told the girl that to be popular she should learn the words to all the current songs. The poor child did as she was told, then sang them constantly in a high, squeaky voice which gained her no friends and even less popularity.

I won $10 from the Women's Christian Temperance Union for an essay on the evils of drink, which caused many guffaws among my friends because we all drank beer illegally and too young. Drugs were not an issue in the '50s, at least not in our school.

Mother and Hal took me to the old Town Casino nightclub in Buffalo to hear Tony Bennett sing on my 17th birthday. The nightclub is gone, but Bennett is still singing. My brother Jim and most of his friends had motorcycles which we rode on back-country roads without helmets. We weren't exactly The Hell's Angels, but motorcycles were cheaper to maintain than cars if you wanted to date on Saturday night.

Jim married my good friend Elaine, who taught me to drive, smoke, and drink more upscale libation than beer. Al also married a local girl, Kay, she of the wonderful laugh and great graciousness. Both Kay and Elaine are very important members of our dwindling family. Jim died in 2002.

I worked part-time at the local department store and the dairy bar during high school, partly because the family spent some summers at a fishing camp, Pete's Place, in northern Ontario, Canada. I thought the place was boring and it was ruining my dating life in Westfield to be away from home, so work was the answer.

I also spent several summers at a Lake Erie resort at Mitiwanga, Ohio, baby-sitting John and Helen McCulloch's two sons, John and Arthur. Our cousin, Vic Dix, also a teen, joined us one summer after he had worked for weeks mowing lawns and washing windows to make enough money to buy an outboard motor for his rowboat. He was so proud of the motor. We lugged it to the dock and he attached it to the boat. At least, he thought it was attached.

Unfortunately, he didn't turn the screws and when he pulled the string to start the motor the engine flew off and sank like a stone. We spent the rest of the summer unsuccessfully diving for it.

To this day, Vic finds it difficult to laugh about it…and who can blame him? A few years ago, I drove to Mitiwanga to see what it looked like after 50 years. I had difficulty recognizing the remodeled house, but I did note that a sign by the tennis courts which used to say *White Gentiles Only* finally was gone. There was a similar sign at the gates of the Chautauqua Institution in the 1950s, too. The 1964 Civil Rights Act, which outlawed such nonsense, was a decade down the road.

Cousin Vic, now a retired publisher, asked me why I had bothered to visit Mitiwanga again. I couldn't resist teasing him.

"I went back so I could dive for your motor," I replied, but he still gave me a tight smile of regret.

I graduated from high school in 1953 and it was time to go to college. I was lucky that I graduated because my grades were a mess. The choice at Westfield High School was to major in math and science or major in Latin. I chose Latin because I knew it would help me as a writer—and it has—but I was hopeless in math even with summer tutoring. Things had settled down at home by then, but I loved to party and be with my friends (still do) and being a serious student never occurred to me. I also wanted desperately to get out of that small town by then and be on my own.

The guidance counselor, Miss Moon, said, "Don't worry about going to college. You'll marry well and it won't matter where you go," which in retrospect seems like odd advice from a counselor. I learned typing and shorthand because it would help me as a reporter. I also was influenced by reading long-out-of-print books like *Peggy Covers the News* written by a moonlighting *New York Herald-Tribune* reporter and of course, the *Nancy Drew* mysteries.

I was rejected by several eastern colleges, but I finally was accepted by Stephens College in Columbia, MO, a good choice even if it had the reputation of being only a girl's finishing school. The best thing about it academically was that students could choose the programs they wanted to study without having to waste time on useless required subjects in their freshman and sophomore years.

I immediately entered the journalism program and became news editor for *Stephens Life*. My first assignment from the managing editor was to interview the president of the college, Thomas Spragens. Suddenly, the reality of what journalism entailed hit me.

I called his office and made an appointment with him via his secretary, but when I went to the office at the scheduled time, I panicked. I walked around the quad four times before I could summon the courage to enter his office. He, of course, was very gracious to this college freshman and laid out his plans for the school year without my asking more than a few, probably dumb, questions. I don't remember much about it, frankly, because there have been too many interviews and too many stories in the meantime.

Aside from the classes, I made lifelong friends with young women from all over the country.

Fran Curry, a Dyersburg, TN, undertaker's daughter, taught me the fine art of saving time by washing clothes while taking a shower, which was a lifesaver when I went to Vietnam and water was in short supply. Dottie, Char, Mugs, and I roomed together. Mugs invited me to spend spring break with her family in Fort Lauderdale, FL, and we flew there in a private jet. Her wonderful Danish father, Jens, encouraged me to go on with my career and see the world.

I can still hear the college song:

> *Now, every Stephens girl is quite a treat*
> *She's just 100-per from head to feet*
> *She's got that style, that smile, that winning way*
> *No matter where you go, you'll recognize her, and you'll say*
> *Now there's a girl I'd like to know*
> *She's got that good old Stephens pep and go*
> *And just to look at her is quite a treat, quite a treat*
> *She's a Stephens girl!*

They gave me an Alumnae Achievement award in 1977 and I returned to campus that June to speak at graduation.

I went home for the summer in 1955, then returned to Columbia in the fall with the intention of going to their well-respected journalism school at the University of Missouri. I only stayed two weeks.

I guess I was naive or didn't make the right connections, but I learned upon returning that most of my Stephens credits wouldn't be accepted at the "j" school and I would have to go to Missouri for an extra year to make up credits.

I had missed sorority rush because I had not been advised of it. The Missouri farm boys seemed very declasse to me after Stephens, and I hated being back in that cow town staying in a quonset hut left over from World War II which was being used as a temporary dormitory.

I called home in tears and Hal answered the phone. Mother was in Florida at the beach house. To his credit, or maybe because he was a sucker for tears, he told me to come home. He wired me the train fare and I left on the *Wabash Cannonball*, a train shuttle, for St. Louis the next day, connecting to Westfield where the passenger trains used to stop. Word went around the dorm that I must be pregnant or I wouldn't have quit school, but that was hardly the case.

I spent the rest of the Fall semester at home and transferred to Syracuse University in the Winter semester. Mother returned home furious that I had quit school, worried that I might not return, and asking me if I WAS pregnant. I was insulted.

She told me that I better get a job because she wasn't going to have me sitting home for four months rotting away. Talk about overreaction. I went to work in a local dress shop, kept a low profile at home, and left for the university in late January.

A few years ago, the Missouri School of Journalism wrote to me and asked that I leave them my journalism papers when I die. It pleased me to write back and point out to them that they hadn't accepted me when I applied to their journalism school and I felt no obligation to give them anything but my best wishes. Someone in the dean's office wrote back apologetically, observing that it was tough for women to gain a foothold in those days. I remain unmoved.

My friend, Helen Thomas of Hearst Newspapers, who had a similar request from them, said, "What am I going to send them? My old notepads? If I can't read them, how could they?" The transfer to Syracuse as a college junior was a good experience. I entered the journalism school with a minor in political science and economics, worked as a reporter/writer on the *Daily Orange*, and pledged Delta Delta Delta sorority. The old journalism school, The Castle, was torn down some years ago and is now the front gate to the Carrier Dome athletic complex.

The Newhouse newspaper family gave the school an impressive communications building that enhanced the school's reputation enormously. As noted earlier, I worked on the Wooster paper during those college summers.

I lived in the sorority house my senior year, a large lovely house on the campus with study rooms on the second floor and a dormitory on the third floor where everyone slept if they could stand the chill. To avoid colds and germs in such close quarters, the windows were never closed. One night, I put my alarm clock on the window sill set for an early class. The temperature overnight dropped to 23 degrees below zero and the alarm clock froze in place at midnight. I was late for class.

I worked part-time at Kupperman's Jewish restaurant in Syracuse for a month until I got fired for dropping and breaking a loaded tray of dishes on the dining room floor. It was heavy work. Old Man Kupperman, who operated a gay bar on the premises at night, would only allow the wait staff to eat borscht from the kitchen for our meals. It was better than nothing, but not much.

I quickly developed a blazing romance with an ad salesman from radio station WFBL that operated in quarters above the restaurant. He was a nice person, but he was in his 30s and ready to marry. I wasn't.

As my senior year drew to a close, it became time to think about serious work. I got offers from several publications including the Macy chain in White Plains, N.Y. which offered me a beginning reporter's position. Mother thought I should take it because I might marry well in that affluent area.

However, Ray Dix, offering me advice from Wooster, said he thought I should "think big" and consider working for one of the wire services which provided news to the media worldwide.

I applied to the Associated Press in Albany and was accepted. The Wooster paper and other Dix publications bought the services of United Press (later United Press International). I applied there, too, and no doubt because of the family influence I was offered a job in Columbus.

In fact, I was sitting on a window seat on the second floor of the sorority house on Friday griping to my "sisters" about the final exams we had just taken when I received a long-distance call from the Columbus bureau chief. He told me that if I could be in Columbus by Tuesday, I could have a job. I never did figure out why he put such time pressure on the offer because he had a large staff, but I accepted. I packed, drove to Westfield with friends, repacked and left by train for Columbus on Sunday. I read Sloan Wilson's *Man in the Grey Flannel Suit* on the seven-hour train ride.

Dressed for a "Flapper Party" in the '50s.

4

NEW JERSEY
Queen of the Statehouse

Since I left Syracuse before grades were posted, my recurring nightmare for years involved failing to get my Bachelor of Arts degree and having to quit United Press because I wasn't as well educated as everyone else. I discovered during my 16 years of employment with them that several of the top executives didn't have college degrees, so it was a ridiculous dream.

It is not necessary to have a college degree to be a good reporter and writer, but Mother's lectures on the need for education apparently invaded my subconscious.

Finally, I awoke one morning when I was working in Washington, after a long dream-filled night, and I thought "okay, I did graduate. I am working. No more dreams." Never again did I have one on that subject.

Actually, it's hard to believe that I wanted to work for UPI so much that I had dreams about it. The hours were long and the pay was poor compared to other businesses, but it was always fun and challenging. We remain like a big fraternity, although UPI essentially is gone, the victim of changing times and greedy ownership.

The Columbus bureau was located on the second floor of the old *Columbus-Citizen Journal* building, a dingy firetrap in the downtown area near the state Capitol building. The dirty windows faced a solid brick wall across an alley with little daylight filtering into the two rooms we shared with Scripps-Howard Newspapers. We didn't write with quill pens, but it was like a scene out of a Charles Dickens novel.

Since I was the first woman they had ever hired in the bureau, there was considerable joking that I probably would hang lace curtains at the windows. I wouldn't waste the lace.

I made $63.65 a week in 1957 and my take-home pay was $53.54. It was equal pay for equal work. I was paid as poorly as the men under the Wire Service Guild contract.

I lived at the YWCA around the corner, common practice for proper young women who needed an inexpensive, temporary place to live. To save money, I shared a double room with a strange girl who wanted a roommate to share expenses. I awoke the first night to find her standing next to my bed, either about to rob me or get in bed with me. I moved the next day to a single room and gladly paid the difference.

The bureau chief who had hired me prided himself on running a training school for young reporters, which he did tactlessly and sarcastically, but we learned a lot. He wanted to be liked by his staff, but he was difficult to please.

One day soon after my arrival, a young black man from the Ohio State University journalism program stopped by seeking work. He was neatly dressed, appeared intelligent and polite. "I have nothing for you," the boss told him.

"Gee, Chief, why didn't you at least interview him?" I asked innocently, after the job seeker left.

"Why should I waste my time and his?" The boss replied. "The only job I would give him would be to sweep the floor."

It was that day that I realized how pervasive discrimination was in the workplace. It was long before the Equal Employment Opportunity Commission was established.

There were about 10 of us in the bureau, several new hires with me, doing menial tasks such as "making books." Six sheets of white paper with five sheets of black carbon paper made a book that was used by the writers to deliver their stories to the desk men who would edit and distribute the pages for transmission on the teletype machines to media around the state and nation. The advent of computers made teletype machines obsolete and put a lot of teletype workers out of jobs or into retirement.

The bureau chief chided Norm, another staff member, one day for wearing a dark shirt to work instead of a white shirt and tie. Norm was taking his turn making books and the carbon paper was smearing on his hands and clothes.

"I don't wear a white shirt to work in a coal mine," Norm snapped at the boss before walking away.

After a few weeks on the job, I was assigned to work the local radio desk which supplied news, weather, and sports reports to the Columbus media. I worked the 6 a.m. to 3 p.m. shift five days a week, Christmas and New Year's, with two weeks annual vacation. I thought I was lucky.

Unlike newspapers and magazines, radio and television writing requires short, one-thought sentences because the spoken word is more difficult to deliver than to visually read a sentence. An on-air spokesperson can be left gasping for air if the written sentence is too long. Another hazard is the double entendre. One of the more infamous weather forecasts began "Jack Frost poked his icy finger into Virginia today..."

Dick, an elderly teletype operator who worked with me, would pick me up at my apartment in his car (I had moved in with another working girl by then) at 5:30 a.m. and we would open the bureau, just the two of us.

One day, Dick emerged from the men's room clutching his trousers.

"The zipper on my fly broke and I can't sit down to type," he said. "Do you have any safety pins or a belt?" I tried not to laugh,

53

but I didn't know what to do. We were ready to start transmitting copy for the early morning radio news, it was still dark outside, and no one was around to help.

Thinking fast, I ran into the ladies' room, dropped a dime in the sanitary napkin machine, and emerged with two safety pins included in the package. Dick fixed his britches and we continued on schedule. If the public only knew what goes on behind-the-scenes to get the news on the air.

No reporter worth the name got out of Columbus without doing a story or a few lines on Sam Sheppard, a once-prominent doctor who was convicted of murdering his pregnant wife in Bay Village, Ohio, near Cleveland, and blamed it on a "bushy-haired stranger" who had invaded their home while the doctor was asleep. He served 10 years in Ohio State Prison in Columbus for the crime, always maintaining his innocence. The trial created a media frenzy at the time.

I covered one of his periodic parole hearings and later, when the case went to the U.S. Supreme Court on appeal, I went full circle and covered that, too, when I worked in Washington. Long after the doctor died, his son worked to clear his father's name, producing evidence that a workman at the house actually had committed the murder, but it was too late for redemption.

The old state prison was only a few blocks from the bureau. It was dramatic on the night of an execution when the lights in the neighborhood offices would flicker and dim as the volts were administered from the electric chair.

"Just like throwing raw hamburger on a hot griddle," someone would invariably say and then laugh. Reporters and medics have an irreverent sense of humor, usually to ease the tension of the moment.

It was a given that if you showed promise in the first five years of employment, UPI would promote you and try to give you a better destination from which to work. Since several of us wanted to work in New York and Washington, the news capitals of the United States, we set our goals accordingly.

As the months went on, I was given increasing experience covering state legislative hearings which would serve me well in Trenton and Washington. I stayed two years in Columbus until I threatened to quit if UPI wouldn't transfer me to New York.

I got second or third prize—Newark, New Jersey.

It was a hoot to work in New Jersey in the late 1950s and '60s. The remnants of the Frank Hague political machine were still operating in Hudson County, across from New York City. Jersey City was a hotbed of crime and corruption. When Hague died in 1956 he left an estate of more than $5 million and several homes, including one in fashionable Palm Beach. He only made about $9,000 annually as mayor.

Mysterious men frequently were fished out of the bottom of Raritan Bay with their feet planted in solid cement blocks. Oil refineries caught fire in Bayonne, spewing flames in the air that could be seen for miles, causing viewers to say "I thought the world was coming to an end."

Newark was corrupt, too, although the police managed to keep the lid on there, more or less, with payoffs from corporations who wanted to do business there. In the '70s, Newark Mayor Hugh J. Addonizio was convicted of extortion and conspiracy.

In a rare burst of morality, local cops in the upscale, suburban Oranges began pounding on the doors of private citizens in the middle of the night to arrest them for OVERDUE library books. They actually took little Johnny and his sleepy father or mother to the police station for booking at 3 a.m. Bail meant return the borrowed book and pay the few cents for overtime. These Gestapo-like tactics went on for a few weeks until the media made such a joke about it that even the librarians were embarrassed. But yes, they got the books back on time.

The Newark bureau was several cuts above the Columbus operation, working out of a standard high-rise next to the Essex House Hotel. My friend and colleague Joan and I drew the early shift again to serve radio and by then, television stations. We were regularly stopped by the police when we were on the way to work at dawn either because they were bored or because we might be prostitutes going home from work, heaven forbid.

Joan got tired of the harassment finally and invited several cops to the bureau to see for themselves that we were legitimate employees. They came. Then she started dating a couple of Newark's finest and they would give us rides to work in the patrol cars. We accepted because it was safer than walking the streets before daylight. It wasn't safe after daylight either, but at least we had armed guards.

It is hard to believe that many of those towns have become "yuppie" enclaves of renovated apartments and houses by a younger generation who can't afford New York City real estate prices.

Gar Kaganowich (who was bureau manager in Newark and helpful to me in recalling stories) remembered the election night that Joan stayed at the hotel next door, and decided to wash her underwear and drape her bra and pants on the window sill to dry. She watched in dismay as a breeze from the open window wafted the garments to the bald head of a man standing below on the sidewalk. He looked up, but Joan was too embarrassed to lay claim. Wearing a tight sweater, she worked election night with her arms folded over her ample bosom. The young college men we had hired to help us count votes took great delight in trying to get Joan to uncross her arms, but she was having none of it. She manned the telephones hunched over all evening so she wouldn't have to move. In those days, we got election returns over the telephone and added them up on an old-style adding machine before transferring the figures to giant white cardboard sheets by hand. No exit polling or computer projections for us.

In a recent column for Media General, John Hall remembered how we called the gubernatorial election in 1961 for Richard J. Hughes, then an unknown lawyer, based on fragmentary returns from populous Essex and Hudson counties. Even Hughes didn't believe us and personally called the office to check. But we had good contacts and we were right. "Flying by the seat of our pants," Hall called it.

There also was the story of an heiress who got cold feet a few days before her society wedding and went missing. Her car was found by the police at Newark Airport, but her family, friends and the authorities had no clues to her whereabouts, although foul play was not suspected. The story was front page news for a week with speculation that perhaps she had been kidnapped.

After several days, we were running out of new material and the police were out of leads. Then Gar had a bright idea to keep the story going.

"Maggie, why don't you go out to the airport and see if you can get kidnapped; see how hard it would be to simply disappear?" I looked aghast, but anything for a story. Gar gave me cab fare and I took off. I returned several hours later having discussed the matter with the airport police, looked at the lighting, the entrances and exits, nearby telephones and a few airline operations.

I wrote a story that it would be difficult to get kidnapped at the airport, a much smaller facility back then, without someone seeing her, but what did I know? Newspapers and other media were hard up for copy, so my story received wide use. Gar was pleased,

UPI was pleased, and so was I. The runaway bride showed up a day later in a Midwest city, returned home, and married the man. She was always going to get married, she said, but she just wanted to have a little fun first.

While runaway brides, or even grooms left at the altar, are often the subject of media scrutiny the issue reached a new high—or low depending on your viewpoint—in 2005 when a woman staged her own kidnapping in Georgia only days before a big wedding to her fiancé. The couple received a reported $500,000 and a book/TV deal for her disappearing caper while the court sentenced her to probation and community service.

I transferred to the night shift in Newark after a few months, working 3 p.m. till 11 p.m. or midnight depending on how busy we were. I was joined by a Princeton graduate named Fred who was gaining experience and money while he wrote books. Our routine was to finish the shift, go around the corner to a bar for a few drinks, then take the train into New York City for breakfast in Greenwich Village. Then, we would either crash at Fred's place in the West Village or I would take the train back to Newark, again to my YWCA lodging, sleep for a few hours, then go back to the bureau. It was a grind, but we were young and we didn't care.

At the end of the year, Norm Cafarell, who was a UPI business representative for the region, asked me to transfer to Trenton, the state capital, to cover the Legislature and become the Bureau Manager. He said it would be "innovative" to have a woman in that position. He liked me, and he thought I could do the job. And by the way, I would get $10 more in my paycheck every week. I guess I should have been insulted at the amount, but I was excited at the opportunity. I was one of UPI's first women bureau chiefs.

I moved downstate to Trenton to head a three or four-man operation—and the key word is man. Two of them promptly quit because they thought that they were in line to become bureau chief and they didn't want to work for a woman. I respected their decision because, honestly, if they were going to undermine every decision that I made, I didn't want to work with them either. Throughout my career, I got tired of hearing "You may be good, but you'll never be as good as your predecessor" or "I miss Tom, Dick or Harry because HE was really good."As the song says, they didn't promise me a rose garden. I tried to run the bureau as a team effort, and it worked generally.

There were many good stories to cover in Trenton and I liked living there. New Jersey actually takes a bum rap as a state because most people see it only as they drive through from Washington, Baltimore or Philadelphia en route to New York. Calling it "The Garden State" may be overstating it, but it is an area of mountains, seashore, many nice towns, and even rural sections.

Also, it is small, the roads are good, and mass transportation is available. My mother would say that I sound like the Chamber of Commerce, but geographically, it is a nice place.

I covered the gubernatorial administrations of Robert G. Meyner and Richard J. Hughes.

An ongoing story which gave us all embarrassment was Helen Meyner's efforts to have a baby and Betty Hughes mothering nine children and having a tenth child while her husband was governor.

Helen, who was nearly 20 years younger than the governor, was constantly rumored to be pregnant. It fell to me to call her at the governor's mansion in Princeton to check it out and I dreaded to make the calls on such a personal matter. She was unfailingly polite, but she never had good news.

"If I am expecting, you'll be the first to know after Bob," she said laughing, but I knew that it hurt her. When Dick and Betty Hughes moved into the mansion, they had nine children (his, hers and theirs) so I felt relieved that I wouldn't have to make the call. Lo and behold, they had a boy during his administration and I missed the announcement because, after striking out with Helen, I had ignored the rumor.

When Meyner was governor, he ordered the portrait of former Governor Harold G. Hoffman hung behind an open door in an anteroom. In order to see it, the door had to be closed and it rarely was. Hoffman, a governor in the mid-'30s, was convicted of embezzling. He was being blackmailed by an associate.

The bad '60s, as they were called, saw the fall of many public servants in New Jersey, some of them quite charming to know personally but guilty of breaking laws. The late Congressman Cornelius E. Gallagher, who had served his country during the Korean War and had risen to become the ranking Democrat on the House Foreign Affairs Committee, pleaded guilty to income tax evasion charges and received a two-year prison sentence and a hefty fine. In the late '70s, U.S. Senator Harrison A. Williams and Congressman Frank Thompson, both New Jersey Democrats, became ensnared in the Abscam bribery scandal and served prison time. Thompson, who maintained his innocence, was convicted of accepting a $30,000 bribe from undercover FBI agents.

When old New Jersey media types get together to reminisce, we count on our fingers (until we run out of digits) the number of potentially good public servants we knew who fell from grace and power. Greed and arrogance was the underlying cause as it has been since the beginning of civilization.

The press corps who covered the Statehouse in the late '50s and early '60s were a close group and we socialized together. The UPI bureau was in the basement of the Statehouse with the back steps to the building outside our window. Both Meyner and Hughes used to stick their respective heads in the window to give us any last quotes or exchange jokes before they went home for the night. It was a very friendly atmosphere.

I could have stayed in Trenton indefinitely and reigned as "Queen of the Statehouse," but I still had my sights set on Washington. It was during that period that I became friends with Helen Thomas, UPI White House bureau chief and now a columnist with Hearst Newspapers; Frances Lewine who worked for the Associated Press in New Jersey and was so respected that she could have run for governor herself; Julius Frandsen and Grant Dillman, who headed the Washington-UPI operation; and executives H. L. Stevenson and Roger Tatarian in New York.

John Hall likes to recall the time he summoned his courage to ask Frandsen for a pay raise to support his young family. John had rehearsed the remarks carefully and concluded, "I would at least like to buy my wife a new dishwasher." Frandsen gazed out the window and said, sadly, "My wife doesn't HAVE a dishwasher." End of conversation.

I went back and forth to Washington and New York with some regularity and became personal and professional friends with all of the bosses. They mentored me and when they felt I had gained enough experience to go to Washington, they made it happen.

Helen Thomas and I have remained loyal friends for nearly 50 years and we see each other often. Her advice to me has always been, "You better do it. It will look good in your obituary." Right.

I covered my first political convention in Chicago in 1960 when Republican Richard M. Nixon received the nomination to oppose John F. Kennedy for President. Al Spivak, a UPI White House correspondent, passed through New Jersey with a group of other reporters after the election to cover Kennedy at Hyannis Port, MA. They invited me to join them at the Yachtsman Hotel press headquarters for the weekend, so I did. Also in the group was the highly-respected and famous Merriman Smith, who won the Pulitzer Prize for his coverage of the Kennedy assassination in 1963. Mr. Smith and the others were very kind to this young reporter on that long ago weekend.

I repaid Al's hospitality and friendship in 1962 when he and a group of UPI friends joined me at a house I had rented for the summer at Belmar on the Jersey shore. I remember that it was August 5, 1962, the day actress Marilyn Monroe died, and we were in deep mourning for the loss of that beautiful Hollywood star.

Al remembers it better as the day I wrote my initials with my finger in the dust on the door of his new car and the sun embedded the design in the paint job, causing a certain strain in our friendship.

When the Bush administration allegedly blocked coverage of the coffins of U.S. troops in Iraq being returned to Dover Air Force Base in Delaware, I was reminded of the countless Saturday nights I spent with a photographer at Dover or McGuire AFB in New Jersey waiting for military coffins to be returned there from around the world. I always felt it was important for the American public and politicians to see how war affected young lives and destroyed entire families. If the photos and stories upset the decision-makers, perhaps it will make them consider the consequences of their dubious actions in the future.

I transferred to Washington in 1963, the year that Kennedy was assassinated. I was dating two men when I left Trenton after nearly five years. They both followed me to Washington, but if timing is everything in life, our time had passed.

Going through the East Room receiving line at the White House on Dec. 12, 1968 shaking hands with President Lyndon Baines Johnson. The Emir of Kuwait is at the left.

5

WASHINGTON
Making My Mark

I f you were alive November 22, 1963, do you remember where you were and what you were doing? Most people do. Books of recollections have been written about it and the anniversary is noted by his family and the media every year. John Fitzgerald Kennedy, our nation's 35th president, was fatally shot while riding in a motorcade in Dallas, TX. People around the world saw the drama and the aftermath unfold on television.

I had been in the Washington bureau only since January and my contribution to coverage of the story was minimal. I learned about the assassination while listening to the radio in the parking lot of my apartment building in southwest Washington. Congress had adjourned late that year and UPI staff vacations were delayed. I had driven home from Capitol Hill to pick up my packed suitcase for a vacation in Puerto Rico with my good friend, Grace Bassett.

I simply pulled out of the parking lot and returned to the Senate Press Gallery. Calls were jamming the switchboard from congressmen and their aides wanting to know what had happened and to express their sadness. I can remember thinking how hypocritical much of the reaction was because many of those politicians had been super-critical of the president and his programs 24 hours ago. They wanted to be on record with the media expressing regret at the death because, as one GOP congressman said to me, "I liked Jack personally. It was his political views I disagreed with, and we'll have to work with his successor tomorrow."

I called Julius Frandsen in the downtown bureau and asked him what I should do. He told me to go ahead with my vacation plans, but since I wasn't leaving for San Juan until after midnight on the "pigs and chickens flight" (in those days, travelers going home to Puerto Rico often carried live animals in boxes on the late flights), could I go to the Elms in northwest Washington to cover the return of now President Lyndon Baines Johnson and his wife, Lady Bird, to their home from Dallas?

Dozens of reporters were already stationed outside the estate when I arrived and there were several portable phones set up, attached to the trees or lying on the ground. I stayed at the site until near midnight when Mrs. Johnson and her press secretary Liz Carpenter drove into the property and entered the home without speaking to the media. Johnson was at the White House. I phoned the UPI desk downtown to relay this information and left for the airport.

In Puerto Rico, strangers would approach Grace and me on the street to offer condolences, windows were draped in black, flags were at half-staff, and photos of Kennedy and his family were prominently displayed in the hotels, offices and homes. It was a tragic time, one of many tragedies for the Kennedy family.

I joined the UPI congressional staff from Trenton to work as a member of the regional team covering politics and government for Ohio, Pennsylvania, New Jersey, West Virginia, Maryland and Delaware, the so-called Middle Atlantic states. At that time, newspapers, radio and TV which bought the UPI and AP services were willing to pay extra to have specialized Washington coverage of their congressional delegations and federal agencies because it was cheaper than maintaining an office there. For newcomers to Washington reporting, it was a good learning experience because we had a continuing variety of stories to cover all over town.

The group were very professional journalists who had distinguished careers and remained loyal friends including Mike Posner, Dan Rapoport, Steve Gerstel, Roy McGhee, Bill Eaton, and Maggie Davis. We worked hard and we laughed a lot. It's not hard to laugh covering Congress where there are 535 diverse personalities with their own agendas and egos. Everyone has a lot to say, some of it not always intelligent but always self-serving.

Since West Virginia was part of my beat, I traveled to that state to see a coal mine operation in action. The United Mine Workers Union said that I was the first woman since Eleanor Roosevelt to go down in a coal mine. It was considered bad luck for the miners for a woman to be present. I tend to be claustrophobic and I didn't like the experience any more than the miners did. They are very brave men. Fortunately, the visit only lasted about 15 minutes…never again.

The race riots and demonstrations in major cities nationwide in 1963-64 before the passage of civil rights legislation caused major turmoil in the nation's capital. Fires erupted in many areas of the city and looting was rampant. At one point, I stood in the UPI offices on the third floor of the National Press Building and watched looters smash the large glass windows of the upscale Julius Garfinkel department store across the street snatching clothes and even hauling off naked mannequins from the window displays.

My college friends, Mugs and Frank Klapperich of Winnetka, IL, had brought their children to Washington to see the sights on Spring break. When their hotel restaurant closed because employees couldn't get to work, they came to my apartment for lunch. The grocery stores closed, too, so I recall serving them creamed eggs on toast because I was low on food. We did find a bottle of champagne in the back of the refrigerator, so we made an event out of it while sadly watching the chaos below.

No matter where I have lived or traveled around the world, I have always returned to Washington at least once a year, often more. My closest friends are there, my work has often centered there, and I have always felt at home there. However, I say that with the caveat that Washington is a "company town" and you are only recognized for your current job—not the one you held yesterday or might hold tomorrow. The phone book is filled with the names of former this or former that. They don't go back to Keokuk after they have worked in Washington, at least not happily. For all its vagaries and foibles, it's an exciting place to be even in its insularity.

I worked on the Hill for nearly eight years until I went to Vietnam, so there are many stories, but you will be relieved to know that I will only tell the ones I found amusing or interesting.

One UPI reporter, hearing advice from a U.S. Postal Service public relations man on how to write a postal story: "You don't tell me how to write a story and I won't tell you how to lick stamps."

A staffer at the Small Business Administration suggested that I bring over 9 or 10 reporters to do an overall series of stories on the accomplishments of the SBA. My answer: "Are you joking? We didn't send that many people to cover World War II." (My bosses, always short-staffed, quoted that exchange around the press club bar.)

Sen. Thomas Kuchel, R-CA, and his wife played bridge with the elderly Sen. John Sherman Cooper, R-Ky., and his wife, Lorraine. "It's funny when we are bidding a hand," Kuchel related. "Lorraine can't see the cards and John can't hear the conversation, but we laugh together anyway."

The late Sen. Stephen M. Young, an Ohio Democrat who didn't suffer fools gladly received a letter from a constituent complaining that the First Lady's horse had been transported at public expense and wanted the same thing for himself. In a letter, the senator replied: "Am wondering why you need a horse when there is already one jackass at your address?"

The famous World War II General Douglas MacArthur died in the Spring of 1964 of acute kidney and liver failure. It is customary in Washington and other world capitals for the leaders to have state funerals which are planned well in advance with input from the future deceased.

In William Manchester's book *American Caesar* he said that MacArthur, who was fired in Asia by President Harry S. Truman, would have gloried in his own funeral. "He had drawn up plans for it, of course," Manchester wrote. "He planned everything. But his instructions for the plain GI casket to the ribbonless blouse had been uncharacteristically modest..."

The open casket was placed in the great rotunda of the U.S. Capitol where a military honor guard was stationed overnight as hundreds of people streamed into the building to pay their final respects.

Meanwhile, upstairs in the Senate Press Gallery we drew straws to see who would take turns on the 24-hour "casket watch" for the old general. With my usual good luck, I drew the midnight-to-dawn shift which meant standing aside watching the crowds pass by in the cold, poorly-lit rotunda. My writing would be part of the main story describing MacArthur's life and the tributes to him.

I gulped when I "won" the short straw, but I wasn't going to admit that I hate funerals and it was spooky in that rotunda. Several things went wrong at the scene. The deceased had jaundice during his illness which gave his skin a yellow pallor.

Because the tribute was televised, the guards closed the rotunda to the public several times so the funeral director could put additional rouge and lipstick on the body to make it more telegenic. One of the high-powered TV lights came crashing down on the dead man's face, burning the flesh before the light was retrieved. Several visitors fainted in the emotion, or turmoil, of the evening. It was a busy night.

I had been on duty several hours when out of the night came Steve Gerstel, the Senate bureau chief and my longtime, adored friend.

"I thought you might need some help," he grinned, producing a Thermos of coffee spiked with brandy and a desk of cards. We retired to the floor behind one of the giant marble columns and played gin rummy till the day shift came on.

As MacArthur said in his farewell speech to Congress, quoting an old military ballad, "Old soldiers never die. They just fade away."

I covered most of the national political conventions beginning in 1960 when Richard M. Nixon received the Republican nomination in Chicago—and lost the election to John F. Kennedy. In 1968, I was assigned to the contentious Democratic Convention in Chicago when Hubert H. Humphrey received the nomination. I covered both party conventions in Miami in 1972 where Nixon was nominated for a second term opposed by George S. McGovern.

Covering political conventions for the wire services was a highly-coveted opportunity. We worked hard, partied hard, and knew that we were part of history, if only until the next election.

The conventions always were free-wheeling affairs where we worked 16-hour days, tried to find a restaurant open at midnight to serve an intimate party of 25 reporters, and spent a good deal of time flirting with co-workers who might be unattainable back in Washington.

Married or unmarried, out-of-town trips on expense accounts tend to generate a camaraderie which only its participants can explain…or gloss over when talking to their wives or husbands.

I contributed a recollection to Helen Thomas's book *Front Row at the White House* (Scribner 1999) about covering the Humpheys in 1968 which always made us laugh.

As Helen told it:

"Late one evening I suggested to Maggie that it might be a good time for an updated feature on Muriel Humphrey as her husband was about to take the presidential nomination. That convention, as most recall, was marred by riots; police violence against the anti-war protesters in Grant Park. We knew security would be tight at Humphrey headquarters on the twenty-fifth floor of the Hilton Hotel, across from the park.

"To circumvent security, we decided to walk up the twenty-five flights of the indoor fire escape and search for Mrs. Humphrey, figuring no one would be mean enough to throw us out if we made it all the way up the stairs at midnight.

"We started climbing, laughing at how out of shape we were and teetering on our high heels. The air in the stairwell was acrid with the smell of tear gas that had wafted in from outside and our eyes began to burn. But we kept huffing and puffing our way up the stairs and finally reached the twenty-fifth floor…only to be greeted by a giant security guard standing in front of the fire exit door with his arms crossed in front of him.

"He wore a black suit and had a very big grin on his face and told us he'd been watching us scale this Matterhorn of a stairwell the entire time.

"We gasped that we knew Mrs. Humphrey—I think the words 'best friends' got interjected somewhere—but he told us she and her husband had gone to bed and he was paid to keep reporters out of the suite. We asked if we could at least ride the elevator down to the lobby, but he told us to go back the same way we had arrived.

"The next morning, Maggie was covering Mrs. Humphrey at some event and Mrs. Humphrey noticed that Maggie was limping. When she asked her what was wrong, Maggie recounted the story of our nocturnal raid on the Hilton. Mrs. Humphrey said, 'Oh, that's too bad. Why didn't you and Helen simply call me on the telephone? You know I would have talked to you.'

"Maggie mumbled, 'Yes, we should have taken that less strenuous route,' to which Mrs. Humphrey added, 'By the way, the children and I are hiding out at the ASTOR TOWERS.'"

Helen and I considered having *Born to Lose* tattooed across our chests.

At the 1968 GOP Convention in Miami, Isabelle McCaig, a good friend who covered the Justice Department, and I, flew together on the Florida shuttle to cover the nomination of Richard M. Nixon.

As was the custom, the UPI accounting department doled out "generous" $150 advances to each staff member for travel costs and convention living expenses. A car and a driver was to meet us at the airport so that would save money.

After a couple of drinks, Isabelle, and I began exchanging confidences. She told me that she might have to borrow money from me because she had paid the rent with her UPI advance.

"You can't borrow," I said. "I did the same thing."

We counted our cash and determined that we had $25 between us. This was Saturday. We wouldn't get another advance until Tuesday. Somehow, this struck us both as extremely funny and we decided it would be a challenge to live by our wits. When you are under 40 and reasonably attractive, lack of money is a mere inconvenience. We could have asked the accountants for more money before Tuesday, but we had our pride.

Isabelle was confident that Stan Hall, a tall, handsome Texan and an editor at UPI (whom she later married between the Miami Convention and the Democratic Convention in Chicago) would be good for a few dollars. When she told him her sad story, he just grinned. I was certain Steve would save me from financial ruin. Instead, he laughed and handed me a brochure listing convention parties or "freeloads" where complimentary food might be served.

"I know you. You won't starve," Steve said, enjoying my hungry look.

The weekend progressed, and Stan and Steve eventually took pity on us, producing dinner and some cash. Early on Monday morning, there was a knock at my hotel room door. A messenger delivered a white envelope with *The White House* engraved in the upper left corner. Evidently, our need for foreign aid had reached the top echelons of power.

I opened the envelope and counted $100. There was a note in the familiar Helen Thomas handwriting. Unsigned, the note said "You and Isabelle owe me dinner." She was right.

We owed her Big Time. I still do.

We were a close group in Washington and we partied together on weekends, talking shop and complaining about the bosses or the stories we were working on. Reporters love to bitch and moan to each other, probably because no one else will listen and sympathize. I lived on the top floor of a southwest Washington high-rise where we flew kites off the balcony at midnight. Later, I lived in fashionable Georgetown in a ground-floor apartment where the only view outside the bedroom window were the balls of four buffaloes which stand guard at the entrance to the Q Street bridge. Pollution and vandalism have damaged their shaggy, bronze coats since they were created by sculptor Alexander P. Proctor in 1913.

I went to a party at Isabelle's one night wearing a paper dress that some designer was trying to market. Someone spilled a drink on me and the dress disintegrated. Isabelle rushed to my side with tape and safety pins. The crowd cheered. I went home in a bathrobe, which was better than a barrel.

That brings to mind the old limerick:

There was a young girl from St. Paul
Wore a newspaper dress to a ball
The dress caught on fire
And burned her entire
Front page, sports section, and all.

During the Kennedy, Johnson and even the Nixon administrations, there were many evening social events, such as state dinners for visiting heads of state, and also daytime teas, luncheons, and awards ceremonies that had to be covered by the wire services, the Washington papers and others.

Since I had to cover the Hill during the day and Helen was on the White House beat with Merriman Smith and Al Spivak, she and I divided the coverage of the evening events, which often went late into the night especially during the Johnson years because LBJ liked to dance with the ladies.

As reporters, we were expected to dress in long evening gowns like the female guests, wear elbow-length gloves which made taking notes difficult, high heels and carry evening bags. The whole idea was to make us blend in with the crowd and be as unobtrusive as possible.

When I asked a senior woman reporter once what her criteria for success was, she replied: "Have good health and wear comfortable shoes because this job requires standing around a lot waiting for something to happen."

Numerous press secretaries and White House aides never missed an opportunity to tell us to mind our manners, be polite and don't intrude on guest conversations. They insulted us, but we did as we were told or the word would be passed to the bosses that we would be *persona non grata* at the White House if we didn't behave.

It was an expensive beat to be on because no one wanted to show up in the same old formal gown every time and it never occurred to the male bosses to give us an expense account to dress correctly.

However, it also was prestigious to be included in the after-party of a state dinner, so it never occurred to us to complain.

Socializing at the White House has been cut back considerably over the years either because the occupants weren't party animals or the number of media wanting to attend the parties as worker bees has diminished. A selection of journalists now are invited as regular guests because many of them, particularly in television, are stars in their own right.

I will always remember the late performer Sammy Davis, Jr. hugging everyone in sight, as was his habit, after he and his wife spent the night in the Lincoln Bedroom during the Johnson years.

"Imagine me, a little black boy, sleeping in the White House," he trilled to us. Davis later was criticized after he was photographed hugging President Nixon at the 1972 GOP convention, but Davis opened the doors for many people of color before and after civil rights legislation was passed.

Helen and I split the coverage of the two Johnson daughters, Lynda

Bird and Luci Baines, when they were married at the White House. The intrepid Liz Carpenter, Mrs. Johnson's press secretary and our friend, handled the press covering the two glamorous events with the skill of a field marshal and both events came off without a hitch.

Liz came to a party at my apartment one night and Helen passed the word "Liz only drinks champagne." It was the period when Helen Gurley Brown's book *Sex and the Single Girl* was required reading for any woman who wanted to date on Saturday night. One of Brown's tenets was "always have a bottle of champagne chilled in the refrigerator" to charm your date.

Cheap though it was, I produced the bottle for Liz who, of course, drank it.

Thirty years later, I produced a more expensive bottle for her birthday in California and told her how nervous I was when I had to produce the cheaper bottle when she was a presidential press secretary. Never ones to turn down good champagne, we toasted to the old days and long friendships.

I have a 1965 speech that the irrepressible Liz delivered to the American Society of Newspaper Editors meeting in Washington when she talked about her job and Pierre Salinger's job as press secretary to Kennedy.

Salinger once said that the most unreasonable media question he ever received was a 3 a.m. query seeking confirmation of a report that Caroline Kennedy's hamster was ill.

"I can match him," she told the audience, "with queries about the Johnson beagle, Him, and the collie, Blanco." Liz was one of the few people who dared to talk back to the formidable Johnson.

A long colloquy with a reporter ended with: "Where does Blanco live?"

"In the White House doghouse," Mrs. Carpenter replied.

"Is he happy?"

"Yes."

"How do you know?"

"Because I'm in there most of the time."

Two trips with Mrs. Johnson come to mind. One was a Landscape-Landmark Tour in Virginia in May 1965 and the other trip was a farewell visit to the family's Texas ranch four months after LBJ died where she entertained women members of the press corps who had covered his administration.

In her memoirs, *White House Diary*, Lady Bird, who made the nation aware of the need to "clean-up and fix-up" our environment, wrote of visiting rest stops, gardens, Thomas Jefferson's home at Monticello, and the Barter Theater in Abingdon trailed by some 40 reporters from all media who were given complete access to the First Lady. She said that she liked the trip because she could speak to us informally, the dress was casual, and we shared coffee and cookies on the bus ride around Virginia.

The visit to the ranch was bittersweet because we knew it was Mrs. Johnson's farewell to public life, but we had a pleasant weekend sitting around on lawn chairs in the front yard reminiscing with her and touring the ranch. Johnson's grave and boyhood home are up the road from the ranch, visited by hundreds of tourists each year.

My friend, Louise Hutchinson, then of the *Chicago Tribune*, remembers walking through a field of wildflowers at the ranch aware that the Secret Service agents were hovering on the perimeter. That seemed a little odd because we were all friends.

It wasn't us the agents were concerned about.

Several rattlesnakes had been spotted among the flowers shortly before our arrival and it would certainly put a shadow on the visit if one of them had reared its ugly head.

I served as President of the Women's National Press Club in

Washington in 1968-69. The inauguration—a large affair of dignitaries, family and friends—was held at the Smithsonian
Institution's national collection of fine arts.

Because I was still on the regional staff on the Hill, I asked the
two senators from Pennsylvania, Joseph Clark and Hugh Scott, to
swear me into office. Both men arrived highly intoxicated and
managed to giggle and mumble their way through the ceremony
and brief speeches. It was an inauspicious start to a long year.

I wore a short white dress with a blue beaded collar that
Mother had bought for me from her jackpot winnings at a Las
Vegas casino. As was customary, most of us still wore high bouffant
hair-dos made popular by Jacqueline Kennedy when she was first
lady five years earlier.

During the year, we decided to make a tour of Russia and most of
Europe's eastern bloc Communist countries.

The whole trip was a bit of a nightmare because we had joined
forces with the American Newspaper Women's Club to enlarge the
attendance—and 74 men and women signed up to go. As any tour
guide will tell you, that is too many people to take as a group anywhere, let alone to what was then considered a hardship zone.

Several members of the group who were not journalists
dropped out early because they didn't like the regimentation, did-
n't want to meet with the Russians, didn't like the food, lost their
passports, became ill, or didn't like their roommates. The complaints went on and on. I was secretly glad to see them go.

It wasn't quite the trip from hell because we learned a lot and
saw a lot, but I was too inexperienced to be leading such a group
and inept at making speeches, or even giving the translators time
to take my remarks in English and translate them into Russian or
Bulgarian or Croatian dialects. I had only visited Europe once
before on a private visit.

We also spent several days in Poland, Yugoslavia, Bulgaria, Czechoslovakia, Hungary and Austria, a strenuous trip. However, the journalists and members of the arts community we met with were gracious and anxious to know more about our lives in the West in those Cold War days.

I threw the Russian Intourist guide into a decline one Saturday night in St. Petersburg (Leningrad) when I asked to see Tsarskoe Selo, the Tsar's Village, about 15 miles south of the city. I had read Robert K. Massie's book *Nicholas and Alexandra* and I wanted to see the country palace that Catherine had built for her beloved husband, Peter the Great, as a surprise.

The Intourist guide said that a trip to Tsarskoe was impossible. It was not on her official list of approved tourist places because the government had not renovated it since World War II. I argued with the woman, stating that I didn't want to take the whole tour group there, just my mother who joined me on the trip and myself. I said I would rent a car and driver privately.

The guide held firm, but so did I. In the end, she and the tour bus driver took several us for the visit because she said she didn't want American women wandering around her country unescorted. I was the leader of our group and I think she felt it was bureaucratically unwise to turn me down.

It was a lovely estate and well worth the trip, but during the Cold War years flexibility was not an option on either side of the equation and Intourist tried to make sure we saw only what they wanted us to see. And, if truth be known, the guide and driver probably didn't feel like working on Saturday night with a group they had been shepherding all week.

One of the more exciting payoffs as press club president was to actually be invited as a guest, not a working reporter, to a White House state dinner. I drew LBJ's entertainment of the Emir of

Kuwait on Dec. 12, 1968 in the East Room. I wore a formal gown with a cream satin straight skirt and a brown-sequined top and the inevitable long gloves. I also gave silent thanks to my mother and to Stephens College for teaching me the correct fork to use at the dinner table.

We sat at round tables of 10 or 12 in the State Dining Room with the Emir, wearing his long robes and kaffiyeh, sitting at the head table with the president and first lady. I sat next to the widow of the well-known architect Eero Saarinen. She seemed pleased when I told her I was dating an architect and she related how she and her husband worked at their artistic projects all day, but met companionably at the cocktail hour to compare notes of the day. He had died in his early 50s and she obviously missed him.

Some weeks later, Frank Eleazer, the UPI chief covering the House of Representatives, pulled me aside in the press gallery for private conversation.

Frank said that he and his artist wife, Lillian, also had been invited to a White House state dinner and she refused to go.

"I don't know what to do," Frank said, seriously. "Lillian kept me awake all night because she is terrified to go to the White House party and I feel that it is important that we attend. A state dinner only comes along occasionally in a lifetime, maybe never. What can I do to make her change her mind?"

I looked blank, but then I told her what every girl knows, "Get her a new dress, with long gloves to match, and get her hair done so she will feel good about herself."

I thought I had solved the problem, but when he called her at home, she was crying and miserable. He handed the phone to me to talk to her, and I tried, but she kept crying that she had nothing to wear and no money to buy anything new.

"Well, charge it," I finally said in exasperation, after she kept repeating herself, "Or I'll lend you some money. This dinner is important to Frank and you must attend." I sounded like a prison matron.

In the end, Lillian got a new dress, Frank wore a tuxedo, and President Johnson danced with her. She said it was the best night she had ever had, except the night that Frank asked her to marry him.

My year as press club president had its moments because most of the women members hadn't achieved success by being namby-pamby or without ego, but on balance it was a good experience.

One of the sadder experiences I had was with a woman reporter who represented several Colorado newspapers. She was tough-talking, but I think quite lonely. At some point, she started to call me at home, usually after midnight. I never could decide if she was drinking when she called, but I doubted it. At first, I was polite and listened to her rant and rave about the people she covered, her bosses and the unfair treatment she felt she received from other press club members because she represented small publications. The phone calls accelerated to three or four times a week, later and longer.

One night, she launched into one of her tirades, concluding with "I don't get any respect from the press club. I think I'll quit. What do you think about that?"

I tried to mollify her and told her that if she wanted to participate more fully in the club, I could certainly use help on committees.

Finally, she roused me out of bed at 3 a.m. to announce "I'm going to quit the club tomorrow."

Half asleep, I told her that I was sorry to hear it, but it was her choice.

The next day, she mailed the club her letter of resignation, and I never heard from her again.

I suppose that she wanted me to beg her to stay, but she wore me down. I've always regretted the outcome because I think she needed all of us.

The WNPC merged with the National Press Club a few years after my tenure. My photo hangs with the other ex-presidents on the wall of the Presidents' Room at the club.

It is even dusted occasionally.

Interviewing the wife of President Nguyen Van Thieu
at Independence Palace in Saigon, 1970.

6

VIETNAM
Timing is Everything

T he Tet offensive of 1968 was underway, most of the fellows who were covering Vietnam for UPI were coming home because their tours were over and most of them had survived. UPI was running out of people to replace them. H.L. Stevenson, then managing editor of UPI in New York, was talking to some of the men at a cocktail party at the National Press Club in Washington, trying to interest them in going.

I said , "How about me, Coach?"

Stevenson, always one of my favorite editors and a friend replied, "What's a nice girl like you want to go over there for?"

I said, "I don't know, but I think I have a right to be considered!"

He said "Write me a letter," which I did. It was filed away in New York and I forgot about it. I still was covering Congress and some of the regulatory agencies.

One day, in November 1969, my Washington boss, Grant Dillman, called me and invited me to lunch. I had been covering the Agriculture Department on vacation relief and I can remember mumbling to myself as I walked across the 14th Street bridge because I was certain that Dillman was going to transfer me from the Hill to cover hog belly futures and wheat subsidies at

Agriculture. I was prepared to resign if that happened.

After we ordered our first drink at the restaurant, Grant said, "Remember that letter you wrote in '68 to Steve?" I nodded. "Well, how would you like to go?"

"I'd love to!" I replied.

We ordered a second drink to celebrate. I left for Vietnam in January 1970 with a promise from Dillman that I could return to Washington.

My tour was originally scheduled for eighteen months, but I stayed for twenty-one because the military was in the middle of the Laotian incursion and the Cambodian invasion and the start of the American pull-out, and the U.S.-managed reelection of President Nguyen Van Thieu.

Although I was very excited about going to Southeast Asia, I was apprehensive, too. While I considered myself a sophisticated Washington reporter after more than seven years on the job there, at age 35 I had never worked overseas before or been in a war zone. For what it was worth, I was sent there to cover politics, not combat.

The reaction from friends and strangers on my going to the war zone was immediate. My real friends came right out with it. They told me I was out of my mind and should be institutionalized for my own protection. My Catholic friends promised to light candles every day until my safe return.

And I received a stack of sympathy cards from virtual strangers which said, in effect, if I wasn't happy in this life, perhaps I would find happiness in the next life. They implied that I had a death wish. I didn't.

After a few State Department briefings on the war, which didn't enlighten me much, and loaded down with cosmetics, sanitary napkins, and a few dishes (which I was told erroneously were unavailable there), I decided to call Stewart Hensley, UPI's diplomatic correspondent at the State Department and a gentleman we all respected and admired. I didn't know him well, but I called him from the bureau and the conversation went this way:

"Mr. Hensley, this is Maggie Kilgore. As you may know, I am being reassigned to Saigon for 18 months and I need some advice from you. You know the area and you know what I should expect. I would appreciate anything you can tell me."

There was a long pause at the other end of the line. Finally, he started to laugh. "Well, Maggie, all I can tell you is if you are on the pill, just remember that you will gain a day when you cross the International Dateline." Timing is everything.

Thus, armed with advice, a new manual typewriter, and combat boots given to me at a farewell party, I left for 10 days in New York to work on the foreign desk for orientation. My friends thoughtfully made sure that I tried a few joints so that I would know how to smoke pot correctly in Asia. I was a smoker, but marijuana always made my eyes water. I sobbingly said goodbye to my brother Al and his wife Kay because I honestly didn't know if I would return.

I flew to Saigon aboard Pan American Airways via California to see my mother who was a housemother at the Bishop's School in LaJolla and then to Manila with a stop in Guam. I was loaded down with books on the history of Vietnam, which I never got around to reading except for reference, and a faulty tape recorder.

I was met in Manila by the UPI bureau chief, Arnold Dibble and his wife Lee, who had lived in that part of the world for 30 years, were friends of my family, and became my surrogate parents.

UPI gave me a very modest cash advance of $200 which meant no extras, so I carried my worldly belongings in four cheap plaid cardboard suitcases that promptly split open coming down the

87

baggage carousel in Manila.

As we approached the carousel, the Asian baggage attendants were fighting over my spilled underwear and holding my bras up for inspection. I kept thinking of a fellow journalist who alleged he covered the entire Korean War with only one change of underwear in a briefcase and a toothbrush.

I was embarrassed, of course, but Arnold simply turned to his Filipino office manager and said "Take care of it. We'll be in the bar." A mid-morning cold beer tastes wonderful in the tropics.

I stayed with the Dibbles at their well-appointed home in suburban Manila, did some last-minute shopping and recovered from jet lag. Their maid, on orders from Lee, unpacked everything in the suitcases which meant that I had to repack before I could fly on.

Since UPI was like a big fraternity where working colleagues automatically became best friends, several members of the Manila bureau stopped by the last evening and we partied until it was time to leave for the airport the next day. It was expected that the guest bring a hostess gift of all the good office gossip stateside, and I didn't fail them.

Vietnam, even during the height of the war, was a beautiful little country with immense tropical jungles, high mountains and valleys, the Mekong River, rice paddies, lakes, and streams.

There never was a question of starvation, such as occurs in Africa, because sea life is plentiful in the South China Sea. The sea played a role later with anti-war activists who maintained the United States was at war because of the oil located there. Oil companies over the years confirmed that there was, indeed, oil under the South China Sea, but the sea depth made it impractical to conduct mass drilling.

However, as we flew over the land in 1970, bomb craters were evident and Agent Orange/napalm had decimated the forests.

I was met in Saigon by the Vietnamese "Mr. Fix-It" and the

bureau chief, Walt Whitehead. I was the so-called "body replacement" for David Lamb, later a *Los Angeles Times* correspondent, who returned to Vietnam after the war, lived in Hanoi, and wrote a book about it. Lamb and I didn't meet for several years because he left on the plane I arrived on.

Fix-It was the office facilitator responsible for obtaining the needed entry and exit documents from the government or military when the staff traveled out of country, making airport runs in the aging office Jeep, and being generally helpful. He was always smiling, but he spoke little English although he understood it if you spoke slowly to him. He was semi-educated, and he was sly. Unfortunately, he also took advantage of us and UPI.

After Vietnam fell to the Communists in 1975 and UPI, like other news organizations, made an effort to help their Vietnamese employees relocate because of fear that they would be killed for working for U.S. companies, Fix-It asked UPI to move him, his wife and four sons to Hong Kong, which they did. They stayed only a few weeks, however, and asked to be moved to the States because he said they were discriminated against by the Hong Kong Chinese, which probably happened. Fix-It and his family spent a brief time in the refugee camp at Camp Pendleton in California until my friend and colleague Tracy Wood and I obtained their release with UPI's guarantee of a job for him. The company transferred them at least twice more because Fix-It said they were unhappy in the United States. Finally, he and the sons were reported working in a Seattle tire factory, relations broken with UPI.

Some years later, I had a conversation in New York with my former translator, Nguyen Anh Tuyet, who had a successful journalism career covering the United Nations. I asked him why Fix-It had behaved so badly when we were helpful to him.

"He really hated all of you," Tuyet said. "He would smile and do what he was asked to do, but he would mutter and curse all of

89

you in Vietnamese and you couldn't understand him, so he could get away with it."

I lived at the Majestic Hotel, around the corner from the UPI bureau on Ngo Duc Ke street, for several weeks until there was a vacancy at the Kim Do Hotel on Nguyen Hue (Street of Flowers) where most of the staff lived, at least the married ones. The Kim Do was a cheap commercial hotel/apartment house, even in its good days, with a single lift to the floors above, French-style with an open metal cage that clattered and clanged as it rose. If the electricity was off, the stairs paralleled the elevator.

There was a restaurant in the back of the building, a large lobby with a reception desk. The hotel was operated by a smarmy Vietnamese man who usually presided in front of the desk clad in white tennis shorts and a T-shirt, anxious to make as much money as possible from the Americans. He arbitrarily raised the rent with some frequency. On one occasion, when the rent had doubled on Jim and Kathy Russell's apartment in one month, Jim, who headed UPI's audio operations, refused to pay it. Mysteriously, there was no electricity in the Russells' apartment the next day. Jim paid the bill. The lights came on.

In a letter to my family, I wrote: *Saigon is an all right city (of 3 million people) but it looks overall like it needs a good coat of paint. Nothing really has been done here since the French left in 1954. Water is the big problem, polluted and always cold. But the women sweep the streets in this matriarchal society and, as we all know, that is more than New York can claim.*

When I returned to Ho Chi Minh City (Saigon) as a tourist in 2000, I was pleasantly surprised to see most downtown buildings renovated and repainted with mini-malls on nearly every block, upscale restaurants and shops filled with affordable merchandise.

My relations with Walt Whitehead, the Saigon bureau chief when I arrived, were tenuous from the beginning. I got off to a bad start when he took me to lunch at a Vietnamese restaurant up the street from the bureau and asked me if I knew how to eat with chopsticks. Showing off, I said yes and promptly started spearing the vegetables with the wrong end of the sticks. It went down from there.

A tall, chinless man from Wyoming who wore eyeglasses, Walt imparted the information that Vietnamese were terrible drivers because they were near-sighted and most of them didn't wear glasses. When I heard that I was going to be working for this Western cowboy who was single, I immediately thought romance, but it wasn't to be. In fact, he didn't like me much at all and it became mutual.

He clearly saw me as a threat to his authority and he evidently thought my Washington background meant that I was a company spy there to undermine his operations, certainly not the case. He didn't like having a woman in the bureau and his romantic entanglements involved the bar girls at the Melody Bar next door. I am a naturally friendly person and I tried very hard to be friends with him, but he never missed an opportunity to make a disparaging remark about my written stories or my sources.

Walt rotated back to the states about eight months into my tour. I wished him well and I meant it. To my dismay and probably his, we found ourselves sitting side by side on the UPI night and overnight desks when I returned to Washington. We frequently worked an eight-hour shift without exchanging one word. One time I had a question about a computer malfunction and asked him for help. Without looking up from his work, he replied: "You figure it out. It's your problem, not mine." I thanked him for his graciousness. He later left the company.

As I look back through my old UPI tear sheets from newspapers, I have no recollection of some of my writing during the early days of my tour. One piece reminds me that in 1970, Defense Secretary Melvin R. Laird came to Saigon on a fact-finding mission for the Richard M. Nixon administration.

I had known Mel when I covered the Hill and he was a congressman from Wisconsin. A kind and genial man, he gave me my first scoop in Vietnam when he spotted me at the airport upon his arrival, invited me to lunch after his press conference, and spelled out in detail his three-hour meeting with President Thieu. Thieu bluntly told him that South Vietnam could not survive a Communist takeover without substantially more economic aid. He also pressed for assurances that the United States wouldn't cut and run.

Laird also made certain that I was introduced to Ambassador Ellsworth Bunker and General Creighton Abrams, contacts who helped me considerably during subsequent months when I needed to check ongoing rumors or even be included on party lists at the embassy.

Julius Frandsen, head of UPI's Washington bureau, wrote Laird a note thanking him for his kindness to me, saying "She wrote with much warmth and appreciation about how much you had gone out of your way to introduce her" to Bunker, Abrams and others. Laird later left government to head *Reader's Digest* in New York.

We also flew north to a fire support base where he and Bryce Harlow, counselor to Nixon, questioned me about which fruits and vegetables were safe to eat. They both confided that they were battling tropical dysentery, but didn't want to admit it. I dispensed remedies I carried in my purse with the advice if you can't peel it, don't eat it. We have to take care of our leaders.

On a similar military flight to the central highlands, I was determined to be treated like one of the guys and avoid favoritism just because I was a woman. The pilot sent word that I was welcome to ride in the cockpit ostensibly for a better view of the landscape. I refused his offer until finally a nice colonel clued me in that I'd better accept because there were about 115 men onboard who weren't using the open hose latrine system in the tail of the plane because I was riding with them and they were pretty damned uncomfortable. I moved up front.

Nixon's Secretary of State William P. Rogers also came to Saigon. A distinguished lawyer and insider in Washington before he joined Nixon, it was widely rumored that he was out of the loop when it came to foreign policy matters in that benighted administration.

He proved that when Bunker held a news conference for Rogers at his embassy residence. We were told it would be for "background only" with no direct quotes allowed. Security wasn't tight in those days, so I put a tape recorder in my large straw purse, surreptitiously turning it on when Rogers started answering questions. I could have saved myself the trouble. He answered no question directly and the ones he answered made little sense. Playing the tape later in the office, I was hard-pressed to find a lead paragraph that would start a news item.

My competitor at the Associated Press had the same problem and didn't file a story to the New York office. Rogers was a dignified man and at least deserved to know what was happening in his government. He left public life soon afterward before Nixon's downfall.

I was critical of the few dozen U.S. Embassy wives who lived in Saigon during their husband's tours, hiding behind their walled villas, complaining about their Vietnamese servants, and being bored with their lives when they could have put their bridge-playing time to better use simply by volunteering at Third Field Hospital or even shopping in the local markets.

"You mean you actually go around by taxi in this awful city?" One embassy matron queried me one day as she alighted from her chauffeur-driven limousine.

"Well, it's either a taxi or a broken-down Jeep or a bicycle," I grinned. She shook her head in dismay.

I sound like an ingrate because several of them welcomed me to their swimming pools or included me at dinner parties on a regular basis, but even that became tiresome when a pattern emerged of banishing women to an upstairs bedroom in their villa after dinner to freshen our makeup while the men enjoyed their brandy, cigars, and conversation in the air-conditioned living room below, often for up to two hours. Then we would be invited back to join the men, drink ice water, and conclude the evening by 10 p.m.

As a reporter, I always tried to question the women on their lives in Saigon and perhaps to learn a little of the embassy thinking on the war, but the wives didn't know and didn't care about what was happening. They were counting the days until their husbands were reassigned to a good post like Paris or London.

The after-dinner separation of men and women evidently occurred in Washington society, too, until *Washington Post* publisher Katharine Graham put a stop to it when she walked out of a dinner party one night. It was insulting to women, the implication being that the women weren't smart enough to join serious male conversations. Or as one wag put it: Sleep with them, but don't eat with them.

In the same vein, I always was uncomfortable at the homes of Asian friends when the wives would serve the meal but not sit at the table as the hostess. At a dinner party in Dhaka one night, I sat at the table eating with three men while the wife and two servants hovered at the kitchen door watching us, ready to jump when we reached for the butter. It seemed very degrading for them, but they didn't challenge the practice.

I looked forward to the dinners that Ambassador Bunker frequently held to entertain visitors from the United States or Asian countries where the conversation was always good and usually produced a story or information which could be developed into a later story.

Bunker, a gracious aristocrat who was serving his government in his retirement years, was married to Carol Laise, the Ambassador to Nepal, and they would shuttle between Kathmandu and Saigon on weekends. I always remember Carol carrying her purse with her from room-to-room at the Saigon residence like a guest instead of the hostess. She entertained me at lunch at her residence when I visited Nepal and set up an interview for me with Mrs. Abrams, the general's wife, who smartly spent her time in Bangkok, Thailand while Abe was running the war. They were both admirable women.

Friend Barbara Cook and I joined the Cercle Sportif, an old French tennis club in Saigon that had a "wonderful" swimming pool. The trouble was the pool had no filtration system and the water was only replenished on Mondays. By the time the weekends rolled around, the pool had a decided yellow cast to it and unspeakable things floated by that were ignored by the Vietnamese gentry who liked to swim. I asked about the old club when I returned to Saigon, but no one seemed to remember it. I later learned that the Communists viewed it as bourgeois and converted it to a workers' meeting hall. Hope they fixed the pool.

Getting through an ordinary day was challenging. I'd get up and turn on the Armed Forces Vietnam radio station, which was taped for the military and played Simon and Garfunkel's *Bridge Over Troubled Water* at 7:50 a.m. every day. I'd shower with a rubber hose that came out of the wall at the Kim Do, get dressed, and walk six blocks to the UPI bureau. Often I would buy a garlicky soup known as *pho* for breakfast from a street vendor in front of the office.

We would talk over what happened during the night and what assignments we had to cover that day—days that usually lasted 12 or 14 hours. It was a strange way of life because if there wasn't some war action going on, it was incredibly dull. This was true all over the country.

At least when you work for an international wire service that supplies news to newspapers, radio and television all over the world, there's always a lot of writing to do about what had gone on overnight, and that kept us busy.

One of the most discouraging days of my life there occurred when I got up at six o'clock in the morning to fly north to DaNang. We were in a military plane, up there all day and returned to Saigon at dusk. On the way, I got my menstrual period on the plane. I was extremely uncomfortable and it wasn't made any easier by the hot military fatigues I was wearing.

I hitched a ride from Ton Son Nhut Air Base to the Kim Do. I was met at the hotel steps by a large rat. They are fearless in that part of the world and we glared at each other. I stamped my foot and he scooted under the elevator. I walked up to the first floor landing, stepped over a drunken soldier who was sleeping it off on the floor, and proceeded to my apartment. As I entered, my pregnant maid was asleep on my bed, so I didn't disturb her. I stripped and turned on the water in the shower, but the only thing that came out was a trickle of mud and slime. The lights and window fan were useless. Nothing worked.

Americans are so efficient and spoiled, and the Vietnamese never seemed to be bothered by inconveniences we won't tolerate. They had been at war so long they would just shrug and giggle.

When I speak to high school and college classes now, I rarely mention the Vietnam War because I get a blank stare. Every generation has its war, and the students of today will remember the Iraq War because they can relate to it and remember their classmates who served.

The Vietnam War was the first war the United States ever lost. It also was the first war to be televised, which went a long way toward stirring up the anti-war reaction from the public and encouraged the peace demonstrations.

In his first interview after leaving the White House, President Lyndon B. Johnson told CBS-TV anchorman Walter Cronkite that television killed his ability to seek reelection. He referred to the newscasts coming across the TV screens in American living rooms every night that incited nationwide protests against the war.

Johnson also remarked that if he lost Cronkite's support of the war, he would lose the support of the American public, which happened. Terms like "light at the end of the tunnel" and "the domino effect" became part of the national lexicon as the war raged on through the administrations of Johnson, Nixon and finally Gerald R. Ford.

Parallels can be drawn between Operation Iraqi Freedom and the Vietnam War—two small countries that never attacked the United States—but at that time the spread of Communism loomed large around the free world. The military and congressional hawks on the war argued that if Communism took hold in Vietnam it would be only a matter of months before most of Southeast Asia would fall under that banner. Vietnam did fall to the Communists, but the domino effect never happened.

"Those who cannot remember the past are condemned to repeat it," said the early 20th-century philosopher George Santayana. As my colleague and friend, Joe Galloway of Knight-

Ridder Newspapers, wrote when he returned to Vietnam on the 30th anniversary of the end of the war: "To those who fought it, mostly young draftees on both sides, the war was unavoidable, a duty their country demanded of them. To those caught in the middle, the peasant farm families, it was an unending and deadly disruption to their lives. One and a half million Vietnamese perished in 10 years. On the black granite wall in Washington, D. C., the names of 58,249 Americans who died in Vietnam are engraved."

A peace rally at a Buddhist temple in Saigon in 1971.
Note the bamboo shields and short skirt.

7

Southeast Asia
The Reality of War

Early in the tour, I fell hard for an Australian lieutenant colonel who took care of me and and my social life at Australian Army parties for the next year. He told me he was separated from his wife and I chose to believe him. I even followed him to Sydney after he rotated home, but long distance romances rarely succeed. This was no exception. And romances that burn bright in a war zone when the principals are 5,000 miles from home often look different as time goes by.

One night we were in bed at the Kim Do when I heard a rat trap I had set *snap* across the room. I shrieked as the varmint dragged the trap across the room, under the bed, and into the bathroom shower, flopping and squealing. We were both awake by then, but I wouldn't get out of bed. My "'hero" mumbled that something had to be done. He turned on the light, went into the bathroom and picked the struggling rat up by his tail and tossed trap and rat out the window. Those Aussies are tough people. Soon after, we heard a bored MP on duty at the USO next door blast away with his rifle at the beleaguered animal.

Most of the married men in the bureau had their wives with them and we became close friends. Kathy Russell, who was a "senior wife" by the time I arrived, taught me how to shop at the military PX in Long Binh where the news media paid the same prices as the GIs. We also received the same Military Payment Certificates which entitled us to military rations of alcohol and cigarettes. Kathy had her first child at a French hospital in Saigon and they honored me by asking me to be the godmother at the child's christening in the Catholic Church there.

The Vietnamese currency was called *piaster* then and small change was called *dong*. When the Communists took over, it all became *dong*. Jim Russell used to tease me by tearing up the essentially worthless *piaster* and listen to me yell at the idea of destroying any money.

Barbara Cook and her photographer husband Dennis lived in an apartment at the top of the UPI building and we had many parties there, leaning over the balcony to watch the GIs pick up bar girls. ("Hey, GI, you Number One. You buy me tea," they would laugh).

Barbara got bored with the drab white walls of their apartment once and had the entire place painted in bright orange. She found it necessary to store staples like bread or cereal in large tin cans every night to keep the rats and bugs away. Burt Okuley, who replaced Whitehead as bureau chief, coveted the Cook's apartment and claimed it when they left. He was aghast at the "live ones" in Barbara's kitchen. "She never complained," he said, in amazement. For his part, Burt moved to a hotel with room service.

Barbara, a pretty woman who hailed from Michigan, had red hair that she wore waist-length. The Vietnamese children, who tended to be dark brunettes and had never seen a redhead, used to accost Barbara on the street to yank out single hairs as a souvenir.

Barbara and I decided early on not to wear the traditional female dress—the *ao dai* (ow-zye)—because it might offend the Vietnamese to see American women emulating them.

The tight-fitting tops with slit skirts worn over long pants looked glamorous on the small Asian women, less so on large westerners. The *ao dao* essentially has gone out of fashion in Vietnam today because the pant legs tend to get caught in bicycle or motorcycle gears and the women say it is easier to dress in western garb, but it still remains a graceful outfit. Dress for women in Southeast Asia differs considerably from the Muslim countries where modesty and religious demands require female head and body covering.

Catherine Kaylor, an Indonesian Chinese, also was part of our group and remains a valued friend. I learned more about Asians and Asian-living from Cathy than anyone I know. Cathy was married to one of our combat reporters, Bob, who had been a friend of mine in Washington. He was upcountry for weeks at a time and she would get bored, disgusted and worried about him. One time she decided to take matters into her own hands and she called Stevenson in New York.

"Steve, this is Cathy Kaylor in Saigon. Bob quits!"

"Thanks for calling, Cathy," Steve replied. And that was the end of the conversation.

Bob returned from the field a couple weeks later, kept on with his job, and laughed when we told him what his wife had told his boss. The couple moved to Washington when his tour was up and still live there. Bob gave up on reporting some years later and became a successful architect at the age of 50. Bob Sullivan, Barney Seibert, and Joe Galloway, combat reporters who faced considerable danger for weeks at a time and survived, were important members of our little band of reporters.

Barney was a great character and a good friend to all of us. In his 50s, much older than the rest of us in Saigon, he served two tours of duty there for UPI which were the highlight of his life. He weighed nearly 300 pounds, was built like a weighted toy with large hips spiraling into a small upper torso, and he had balding white hair.

Barney was the despair of helicopter pilots because they worried that his weight would jeopardize the balance of the craft. Some refused to transport him around the country, but he was so pleasant and intelligent that the military officers enjoyed his company. He worked hard, traveled constantly, and he was a great reporter and writer.

His comment to me once when he had difficulty finding a flight back to Saigon from some remote outpost was "first you worry about how to get there, then you worry about how to get home." I've thought of that remark often when I am stuck in an airport waiting for a delayed flight.

When his first tour in Vietnam was over, UPI assigned him to Los Angeles. He returned for a second tour only a few weeks later. When I asked him why he came back, he said "I got to Los Angeles and the bureau chief said 'there are only a few good stories here … and I write them.' There obviously was no place for me."

The military in Saigon should always be indebted to Cathy Kaylor and me for staging Thanksgiving dinner in 1970. In fact, we probably deserved a commendation medal. It all started at a cocktail party at the Caravelle Hotel given by one of the television networks in mid-November. There was a large group of military officers there and the conversation inevitably turned to talk of home and family and how they were going to miss Thanksgiving on their one-year tours. Cathy, who had never been to the United States, knew about Thanksgiving hearsay because she had served as social secretary to the U.S. Ambassador's wife in Jakarta before she married Bob.

After a few drinks, we became imbued with the spirit of the occasion and began inviting everyone to Thanksgiving dinner at the

UPI bureau. In the cold light of the next day, we said "Oh my God, what are we going to do?"

Comments were made by various husbands on the staff that if we backed out of the dinner we would "lose face," a definite negative in Asian culture. Initially, we bought four of the largest frozen turkeys available at the Ton Son Nhut Air Base PX on the edge of Saigon.

It never occurred to us to check the size of Cathy's oven and I only had a hotplate and a "cold box" packed with ice for liquids. In fact, I became locally famous for my spaghetti dinners because I could only boil food. Ever resourceful, Cathy made a deal the day before Thanksgiving with the Vietnamese-Chinese chef at the USO next door to cook her turkeys. When I suddenly realized I couldn't cook my birds, I called her in a panic and she called the chef to say there would be four turkeys.

"Okay," said the resigned chef, in broken English, "bring over." He put the turkeys in his industrial-sized oven, and then asked "You got pumpkin pie?"

"Uh, no," we replied.

"So," said the chef, with proper Asian dignity, "No pumpkin pie. No Thanksgiving."

He grinned at our discomfort. Then, triumphantly, he opened his giant refrigerator and produced several dozen pies he had baked for the USO Thanksgiving, popping several in the oven to warm for us. We paid him for his trouble and invited him to the party, too.

In the end, we entertained more than 80 Americans and Vietnamese in the bureau manager's apartment. Guests supplied the Scotch, Cognac and side dishes. Everyone had a jolly time even if we were thousands of miles from loved ones. The last guest literally rolled down the steep curving stairway, laughing all the way. Catherine and I were the talk of Saigon for our hospitality, at least until the next holiday.

At Christmas, one of the photographers posed a GI leading a turkey down the street to its final reward at the USO, apparently to show Christmas in the war zone to the folks at home. After the photo session, he brought the bird to the office where it created havoc—and droppings—until Mr. Tuyet, the translator, took it home to save for his family's Tet celebration in February. The bird thrived in a pen in Tuyet's yard until Tuyet awoke one morning to find the rats devouring it. Tuyet was heartbroken because he had big plans for a family feast, but it wasn't to be. As Tet approached, the office bought Tuyet's family a frozen turkey at the PX to replace the loss.

We spent a lot of time covering congressmen who were "seeing the war" at taxpayer's expense. Many were there just to criticize and some just to observe or get out of Washington, but they were mostly a waste of time for us. I felt the same way the military felt about them—we just wanted to get on with the war and stop having to entertain politicians.

As I said earlier, I essentially was there as a political correspondent, not a combat reporter, covering the U.S. Embassy and the Thieu government and peripherally, the Paris Peace Talks, which went nowhere. I have often been asked if I felt strongly pro or con about the war when I agreed to go. I wasn't being paid by UPI to have an opinion. Wire service reporters are trained to give both sides of an issue, clearly and fairly, because their story coverage is bought by media around the world. If the buying media wants to put a slant to the story, that's up to them.

The contrast between American journalist war reporting and depth of coverage in Vietnam, Laos, Cambodia and now Iraq was considerable. In Vietnam, a press badge or a reporter shouting *bao chi* (press, media) often carried weight in a conflict because we were seen as non-combatants. In Iraq, it frequently was dangerous to be identified with the media from any country as witnessed by the fact that over 75 journalists and media staff had died since the Iraq War began in March 2003 until early 2006, according to The Committee to Protect Journalists, which keeps count.

Correspondents and photographers in Vietnam were able to climb on a helicopter and fly to Danang, where there was a press center set up by the military, or Dalat in the central highlands, or the southern delta, for eyewitness accounts. Certainly Vietnam was a dangerous and difficult place to live and work—as all war zones are—but freedom of movement was possible in most areas of South Vietnam, especially when the U.S. military was still in charge.

The reporters of the time were criticized for covering the war from the bar of the Caravelle Hotel, but that was unfair and untrue. The protection committee listed 66 reporters and photographers who died in Indochina covering the war. There were some 300 reporters accredited by the Defense Department to work there at any given time—about 75 of them were women.

It was grim, sad work to hear that another journalist had "bought the farm" and we would visit his or her apartment or hotel room to empty the closets and drawers to ship belongings home. The military and the American Embassy gave shipping help, but someone had to do the packing. I remember walking over to the Majestic Hotel around the corner from the office to pack Kate Webb's clothes and personal effects when she was captured in Cambodia and held for 23 days. Her ordeal was described in the book *War Torn* (Random House-2002). Kate, a UPI correspondent from New Zealand, was later released, one of the lucky ones to survive.

Vietnam was divided with North Vietnam held by the Communists with infiltration in areas of the south. In Baghdad, the

"Green Zone" where the U.S. Command operated was designed to be safe from attack, but even that section was infiltrated by insurgents and by weapons fire on several occasions.

As General Tommy R. Franks, former commander-in-chief of the U.S. Central Command, who had been in both wars, said on television: "In Vietnam, we essentially knew the boundaries of where the enemy was and where we could go. This is not the case in Iraq where the insurgents seem to be widely spread out and active with few boundaries."

U.S. and allied troops had to learn to be jungle fighters in Vietnam. In Iraq, urban warfare took its toll with roadside bombs and suicide bombers favored as the weapons of choice for the resistance in Baghdad and other populated areas. In Vietnam, Buddhist monks committed immolation to make an anti-war statement with some regularity, but when they killed themselves, they didn't take 100 innocent civilians with them to martyrdom.

I remember one Sunday morning in Saigon when I received a phone call at the bureau from a local monastery telling me that one of their monks planned to immolate himself in front of Independence Palace within an hour. It was such a common occurrence that we almost ignored it, but the monks wanted the media there to make their point about the need for peace. When a photographer and I arrived at the scene, the fellow doused himself with a liquid, presumably gasoline, but the matches he planned to use were wet and wouldn't light. I noticed his hand was shaking uncontrollably. Another monk handed the man dry matches. A photographer standing in front of the monk reached out and knocked the matches out of his hand. The monk, visibly relieved, fainted. We left the scene.

Battles at the pagodas often involved combatants slugging it out with wooden batons while holding up bamboo shields, similar to the sport of fencing. At noon, they would throw down their shields, eat a rice lunch, and take a three-hour siesta. You have to pick your battles to make a statement. I was issued a gas mask when I went to Saigon, but I kept it in the bottom drawer of my desk, unused.

Gloria Emerson of the *New York Times* made her name writing about the orphans of war, the GIs in the hospitals, and how the war affected the man-on-the-street. I followed her lead with as many human interest stories as possible aimed for publication in local newspapers stateside patterned after the work of Ernie Pyle of Scripps-Howard Newspapers during World War II.

Every three months, UPI approved R and R (rest and relaxation) trips out of the country, which were usually badly needed by all of us because we worked seven days a week. We would leave Ton Son Nhut on commercial flights for Hong Kong, Bangkok or Singapore carrying grocery lists for our colleagues and the Vietnamese who couldn't buy special items in Vietnam. It was routine to bring kosher food from Hong Kong for the Jewish correspondents or quantities of nail polish, hair spray and shampoo for the French-Vietnamese woman who operated a beauty shop up the street. She, in turn, would sell many of the products on the black market for inflated prices, but it was prudent to ignore that aspect of her business if you wanted a fast hair cut that didn't make you look like a Marine recruit.

The whole Saigon bureau will always be indebted to the hospitality of Max and Lynn Vanzi in Singapore who opened their apartment to us, fed us well, and entertained us royally. I remember Lynn and me shopping in the Communist Chinese stores in Singapore for great bargains, considered verboten during the Cold War days and before China opened to the West. Max was the UPI Singapore bureau chief who also helped in Saigon.

Late in the tour, I spent two days on the *U.S.S. Constellation*, part of the Navy's 7th fleet, cruising the Gulf of Tonkin, landing and taking off on the aircraft carrier near Da Nang. I was too naive to know that helicopter landings and takeoffs are quite dangerous, especially landings as the carrier bobs around in the sea.

Actually, I found the whole visit rather boring. Sailors onboard have their own routine well-established and they are well-trained, but as an outsider there wasn't much to do but drink coffee and play cards with some of the officers. I was given my own little stateroom and when I emerged in the morning I found a sleepy sailor sitting on the step where he had been sent overnight to guard me from intruders. I was embarrassed to think he had been diverted from his duties for such an unnecessary task, but no doubt it would have been a scandal if I had been mistreated or attacked aboard ship.

I dined with the ship's commander, Capt. John M. Tierney, and was warned by his press aides that I wasn't to mention the war and that I was to let him take the lead in the conversation. Protocol be damned. What a ridiculous admonition to a reporter! However, it was easy to comply because the first thing he asked me was "Tell me how you think the war is going?" The second question was "What is it like, for a western woman, to live in Vietnam?" He listened carefully to my answers. His press aides nearly fainted at his honest curiosity.

I was reminded of a couple of conversations with Admiral John McCain, father of Sen. John McCain, R-AZ, who was genuinely worried about his son being held as a POW at the infamous Hoa Lo Prison, dubbed "The Hanoi Hilton." The admiral, head of the Pacific Fleet based in Honolulu, came to Saigon during my tour questioning journalists closely about the Communist prison. We didn't know much, and surprisingly neither did the admiral, since North Vietnam was inaccessible. His military intelligence wasn't much better than ours. I was pleased to be able to tell the senator about his father's great concern for his welfare when we all returned to Washington, which seemed to touch him deeply.

In the ensuing years, I have been asked if I felt endangered or was injured in Vietnam. Like all of us, I have my war stories.

Once I was in a helicopter in the southern delta, sitting in the rear with a reporter from the *Christian Science Monitor*, and suddenly we noticed it was on fire. We landed and they dropped the back door. As we ran out, we watched it blow up. No one was injured. We rented a car and drove back to Saigon.

Another time I was taken up to the DMZ (demilitarized zone) in a helicopter and we had to exit because there was shooting nearby. The pilot didn't want to land because the ground was marshy and he might get stuck and not be able to take off. As he hovered, we jumped into a potential minefield, ran to the road and jumped on an armored personnel carrier. I jumped, but I missed the vehicle, lost my balance, landed on stones, and broke my tailbone. That was my war injury—and how does one bandage a tailbone?

After nearly two years of living in South Vietnam, it had become a way of life. I wasn't homesick at Christmas because we had already celebrated the holiday, due to the time difference, when celebrations were beginning at home. Comedian Bob Hope entertained the troops at Binh Hoa and we were glad to be included in the audience. Anti-war activists made fun of his traipsing around the world to entertain the troops, but we appreciated having something fun to do on the holidays. My friend Isabelle McCaig Hall thoughtfully sent me a Spiro T. Agnew watch as a present so I would feel in touch with my old life in Washington.

In late 1971, several of us in the bureau were leaving together. The American pull-out was starting, the elections were over, and it was time to go. You can't cover a war all of your life, although some of my male friends never quite got over the experience and lived in a "time warp" for many years. The night before I left Saigon there was a rocket attack and I slept right through it. The war ended four years later. I felt I had done my time, the experience of being over there, being permitted to cover the politics of the war, to travel the world, was a great opportunity. I wouldn't trade it.

It will look so good in my obituary!

First Lady Lady Bird Johnson received the Golden
Candlestick award for outstanding service to our country
at a Women's National Press Club dinner, 12/02/1968.

8

HOLLYWOOD
Time for a Change

I was standing on a Washington street corner waiting for a bus to go to work on a cold, blustery Sunday morning in February 1972 when I thought *I don't need this. I'm going to find another job in a warm climate. I hate cold weather and I'm fond of the tropics.*

I had returned to Washington, traveling through Europe from Southeast Asia, making the crossing on the Queen Elizabeth II from LeHavre, France to New York with my friend Don Thompson of Boston. My luggage from Asia was lost on a flight from Athens to Rome, so I arrived after nearly two years abroad with all my worldly possessions in a brown paper grocery sack .

I stopped in Rome long enough to buy a pantsuit, a long evening skirt and a bathing suit plus toiletries. There is a great case to be made for traveling light. My luggage was in New York when I arrived.

Grant Dillman, the Washington UPI boss, had promised me that I could return to Washington after the Vietnam tour ended, which I did. However, like several of my colleagues from other news agencies, we felt our companies "owed us" for serving time in a war zone. The companies didn't feel that way at all. Their attitude was that they had given us the privilege of working overseas, someone else had to do our work while we were away, and they owed us nothing except a job when we returned.

It was a difficult attitude to adjust to, and personal ego made it more so, which is why I ended up on the night desk editing copy and starting to look around for a better job. There were few jobs at UPI that I hadn't done and I was bored being back in Washington listening to the same old gossip about the same people. It was *deja vu* all over again.

I had covered Congress, been Helen Thomas's backup at the White House, and the women's editor job in New York was already held by Gay Pauley. I considered applying for a position as a UPI business representative selling the news services to newspapers, radio and television stations, but it would mean being on the road by myself five days a week. One of the business reps told me, "You'll get more satisfaction and money selling shoes."

My mother, sister Martha, and brother-in-law Norm had moved to California in my absence, so I decided to join them and leave the cold weather. I was approaching 40, I wanted a job change, and I figured I would never be more marketable as a reporter/editor than I was then.

I applied to the *Los Angeles Times* as a general assignment reporter. It took about six months of flying back and forth to Los Angeles for interviews, but eventually they offered me a writing job on the financial staff. Meanwhile, Dillman had transferred me to the Justice Department at the start of the Watergate scandal in the Nixon administration, so it was a difficult decision to decide whether to go or stay.

Frank P. Haven, the managing editor of the *Times* and a veteran newsman, told me he thought I would regret leaving UPI for the *Times* because, "With your background, I think you will find Los Angeles dull and unsophisticated." He was partly right.

In my fantasies, I always thought I would sob uncontrollably when I finally wrote a letter of resignation after 16 years at UPI, but when I sat down at one of the old manual typewriters in the Washington bureau to formally quit, I wrote it out in two sentences…and never looked back.

I was hired at the *Times* by Rob Wood, who remains my good friend and has had a long and distinguished career in journalism. At that time, he was the Financial Editor on *Fin-Reg*, journalism parlance for *Financial-Regular* editions.

One of my first *Times* assignments was to cover a press conference held by the White Motor Co. of Cleveland, Ohio at the all-male, all-white California Club in downtown Los Angeles in 1973. I went to the club accompanied by a black *Times* photographer, a very professional, dignified person. We were met at the front door by an officious, uniformed attendant who looked at this woman and a black man and stated, "Tradespeople must use the rear entrance."

"We aren't tradespeople," I replied. "We are here to cover a news conference by White Motor."

"No women and no blacks can use the front entrance," the attendant replied, blocking the doorway.

"Look, we don't want membership," I argued. "We were invited to come here."

"You will have to use the back entrance," said the attendant, standing firm. The photographer looked at me and I looked at him. I wasn't going to take that order from anyone, male or female.

"Get out of my way," I snarled, pushing the astonished attendant out of the doorway and proceeding to the press conference with the photographer.

I complained to the clueless White Motor public relations staff who were embarrassed because the *Los Angeles Times* was, and is, the city's leading newspaper. When we returned to the office, I told Rob what had happened. To his credit, and also the *Times'*, an edict came down from management: The newspaper does not cover press conferences at places which practice discrimination.

Times have changed for the California Club and other private clubs, of course, but it surprised me that liberal California was far behind the East Coast in adopting anti-discrimination policies nearly a decade after the passage of the 1964 Civil Rights Act and supplementary legislation.

There was supposed to be a glamorous side to working in Los Angeles, mixing with movie stars, sitting around the pool at the Beverly Hills Hotel interviewing famous producers, and attending the Academy Awards which were off-limits to the mainstream media unless you had a specific reason to be there.

I told my friend Harry Anderson at Paramount Studios that once before I die, I would like to see an Oscar presentation. He called me several weeks later and said "Would you settle for an Emmy awards show?" I struggled into a long formal gown and joined him for a nice evening.

On one occasion, I covered the Hollywood Park annual meeting in Inglewood where the handsome and debonair actor, Cary Grant, was a member of the racing park's board of directors. Tall and tan, he looked as wonderful in person as he did in still photos and movies although he was long-retired.

When the meeting ended, I had a couple of questions to ask the board, so I approached Mr. Grant. Graciously, he said the answers were complicated and would I join him for coffee and he would explain it to me?

I accepted just as graciously, and then looked at my watch. It was newspaper deadline time downtown, I was nearly 20 miles from there facing late afternoon traffic. I had to refuse coffee with sexy, charming Cary Grant, and I'm still bitter about it!

The financial staff was a good group of fellows and, as usual, I was the token woman, not a bad appellation because the men deferred to me and helped me to become a better reporter and writer. It was strange for me, however, not to have my support group of close UPI friends around me, and initially I felt that the newsroom staff was unfriendly and perhaps fearful of keeping their own jobs so they were reticent around newcomers. I never did understand the inner politics of the *Times* where who was eating lunch with whom seemed to matter.

My friend Betsy, the food editor, and her boss, Jean, and I became pals because we had joined the paper about the same time and usually had lunch together in the newspaper cafeteria. *The Times* did add more women to the staff as the months progressed, but to me it was slow going.

One troubled young woman who worked as a copy girl took to eating her lunch in the ladies' room standing behind the door, which swung open frequently, and spilled her food. Several of us felt sorry for her and invited her to join us for lunch, but she refused. She left after a few weeks to go to embalming school near Forest Lawn Cemetery where she said she could get some peace and quiet.

The publisher's wife issued a memo from the executive offices stating that women reporters shouldn't wear pantsuits to work because it was unladylike. She also hired an interior decorator who looked around the cluttered newsroom stacked with papers and junk on desks and issued another memo stating that every desk was to be neat and clean when we ended the workday. However, she apparently forgot her own rule and appeared in the newsroom in a pantsuit. So much for those orders.

With the advent of computers and pods, the newsroom took on the aura of an insurance office with carpeting on the floor and staff speaking in hushed tones. The need for increased security has meant that friends and strangers no longer wander around the halls on an informal basis.

Early on, my main job was to interview corporate heads and write stories about them, but I found it difficult to make the transition from covering politics and public figures to understanding the more private and convoluted world of business. In retrospect, I would say if I knew then what I know now, I would be a lot more valuable to the *Financial* section. If life is a learning process, I've been there.

On my news beat, I also was assigned to cover the Sunkist Growers annual meeting at their headquarters in Sherman Oaks in the San Fernando Valley. Orange and lemon growers are a hardy lot of men and women, invariably sun-tanned from working in the groves for long hours, worrying about growth and overseas competition, the weather elements and earthquakes. They earn their money.

A long-forgotten chief executive officer made his report to the assembled cooperative growers at the annual meeting, concluding gratuitously, "Let's have a big round of applause for our hardworking office staff. Why, some of them come in here at 9 a.m. and often don't go home until at least 6 p.m.!"

The citrus growers, many of whom had been up since dawn tending their groves before leaving for the meeting, just stared at him. He tried again by clapping his hands, but the silence was deafening. He was like a comedian whose joke had bombed. Finally, he filled dead airtime on stage by saying, "Moving right along." Then he told the members how much they were going to receive in payment from Sunkist that year. The applause came, loud and long.

My colleague Bob Rosenblatt likes to recall covering the oil industry in California which included many self-made characters including Armand Hammer of Occidental Petroleum who managed to terrify his office personnel on a regular basis with his demands and eccentricities.

He hired a public relations man, Carl Blumay, but it was never clear whether Hammer, a born self-promoter, wanted to be quoted in the media by a company employee or to speak for himself. Blumay seemed so afraid of the boss that when Rosenblatt called him for a quote on an issue, Blumay would talk to him, then say, "But that's off-the record. And the off-the-record also is off-the-record." It's possible to stay as a company spokesperson for a long time if you never say anything worth quoting.

The Times and also UPI had strict guidelines against accepting gifts and favors from news sources, although many reporters, especially in sports, travel and entertainment, ignored the rules. At the holidays, stories were rampant about sets of luggage, kitchen appliances, and cases of liquor being accepted at a reporter or editor's home from a grateful public relations person who had managed to get a story about his personal or corporate client published during the year. Even today with economic hard times facing many publications, some reporters and editors will accept free trips from a source because they can't afford to travel otherwise. There is no guarantee that a story, favorable or negative, will be written or broadcast, but it is implicitly expected by the host company or government that one good turn deserves another.

I followed the rules, but I had to agree with a chairman of Max Factor Cosmetics who gave me a half dozen tubes of sample lipstick at the conclusion of a *Times* interview. When I told him we were forbidden to accept gifts, his dry comment was, "They insult you, Margaret, if your editors think you can be bought off so cheap just for writing a story."

Later, I kept a dozen red roses on my desk sent to me by a garment industry executive. The flowers died before an editor told me to get rid of them.

In 1976, Wood had been replaced as financial editor by John Lawrence, who I had known in Washington. Lawrence summoned me to his office off the newsroom one day and said that the *Times* had been asked to submit a candidate for a new Ford Foundation Fellowship, the Walter Lippmann Fellowship, a six-month, all-expenses paid program on labor relations which involved travel all over the country. Was I interested? I was.

I never was sure whether Lawrence had submitted my name because I was the most dispensable member of the staff or because he honestly thought it would bring prestige to the newspaper to have an employee on a recognized fellowship.

I flew to New York to be interviewed for the fellowship at the Ford Foundation along with half a dozen other media types from around the country. I can remember being nervous that I might not be chosen disgracing myself and the paper, but I needn't have worried. We were all accepted.

The program was managed by Fred Friendly, who had been producer and confidante to the radio and TV giant Edward R. Murrow, during World War II and beyond. Friendly was proud of his association with the late Murrow and began most of his sentences with "As Murrow used to say..." Lippmann, for whom the fellowship was named, was a prominent Washington columnist and social critic who died in 1974.

I returned to Los Angeles, closed my apartment on the beach in Santa Monica, and left for orientation in Washington.

It was an interesting, if lonely, six months on the road because our little group of fellows were scattered at labor camps for migrant workers in the southwest, Indian reservations, affiliations with labor unions, corporations which had progressive employee relations programs, and stints at the U.S. Labor Department.

Lawrence didn't bother to tell me early on that he expected me to file stories for the paper along the way, so I spent an inordinate amount of time working for him. The other members of the team seemed to spend a lot of time sightseeing. There is no free lunch.

I affiliated with a Native American tribe in northern Wisconsin and slept in a cold, bug-infested wigwam one night, but it seemed an odd place to be studying labor relations when most of the reservation hadn't had steady work in years and depended on welfare.

Later, I stayed at a hotel in Madison at the end of August, near the scenic University of Wisconsin campus, and discovered that I was the only guest. There is nothing quieter than a college campus in late summer.

I called my friend Steve Gerstel in Washington, whining that I was bored and lonely there.

"Oh, for God's sake, Maggie," he replied. "Go down in the bar and pick up some guy. You know how to do it." Since the bar was empty, I wondered who he had in mind.

The overall program was interesting, however, because computers, duplicating machines, and other equipment designed to make a secretary's life easier were coming into widespread office use. No more "making books" for copy like we did in the Columbus bureau and typing on manual typewriters.

I never bought into the theory expounded by labor specialists at that time, however, that the new equipment would make a secretary's life so easy that she could do other chores and move up the ladder of success, breaking through the glass ceiling of advancement for women. A secretary is still a vital part of any office operation and, besides, who will answer the telephones or maintain the fancy equipment?

I returned to the *Times* financial staff after the fellowship was completed and life went on. Since companies come and go with frequency in California, we joked that a successful firm was one that had been faithfully serving the public for at least five years and only been through bankruptcy proceedings twice.

After several months, there was an opening at the *Orange County Times*, which was expanding, and I applied to work in the bureau in Costa Mesa. I usually worked the weekend desk, editing copy and talking to police and fire departments about their casualties in traffic and the nearby beaches. It was very routine.

However, the tour in Orange also was where I flew with the Blue Angels at the now-abandoned Marine Corps Air Station at El Toro and spent an afternoon floating around in a Goodyear blimp which was tethered in Long Beach.

The blimp ride came about because one of the photographers was assigned to take aerial pictures of storm damage to homes built in the canyons and along the shoreline in posh areas of Orange County. I tagged along to take notes.

When I tell children that I took a blimp ride it generates wide-eyed interest, but I actually thought it was one of the longest afternoons of my life. The gondola underneath where the pilot and co-pilot control the craft was crowded with equipment used for lighting nighttime sports events, most of the passenger seats were removed, and we were at the mercy of men on the ground to pull us down with long ropes when we wanted to land.

The pilot confided that the turnover in his job was considerable because of long hours and repetitious flights, but for Goodyear, Fuji, Sanyo and others, it has been good public relations for many years.

And good PR is priceless.

9

LAS VEGAS
A Gamble in Public Relations

In 1979, I decided to leave newspaper journalism and try another branch, public relations. I felt that I was burned out on the day-to-day writing grind, I needed more money, and I generally was unhappy at the *Los Angeles Times*.

With my usual good timing, I had approached an editor about a possible transfer back to Washington. Unfortunately, the day I met with him was also the day that he had asked his wife for a divorce and she refused to discuss it. He was less than receptive to me.

As always, I put out the word to my friends that I was "looking." Soon after, my friends and golfing buddies Chris and Bernie Roswig told me that a casino/hotel company, Caesars World Inc., was looking for someone with a journalism background to head corporate public relations for them in the Los Angeles headquarters.

I was put in touch with the president and chief executive officer who evidently thought he could hire some sweet young thing on the cheap. When he realized that I didn't meet that criteria and carried the prestige of working for the *Times*, he hired me anyway and paid me fairly. He always told me he hired me because I was

Scotch-Irish as was he.

My family and friends were aghast that I would leave newspaper journalism where I had worked for 30 years to join "The Mob." My mother was certain that I would become some gangster's moll on the road to degradation even though I was in my 40s and presumably had obtained some level of judgment and sophistication.

The casino industry has gained an aura of respectability and profitability since the '70s, watched by the Securities & Exchange Commission and numerous state agencies, but at the time I worked there it was still tainted with Mafia connections and a collection of unsavory characters who supplied the industry, such as the laundry concessionaires, the food and liquor wholesalers, even the entertainers.

Gaming has always been an exotic industry that the news media and financial analysts don't quite understand, although they seem perfectly willing to accept free trips to Las Vegas, Lake Tahoe and Atlantic City to "study" the business.

Caesars Palace in Las Vegas prided itself on providing every comfort and convenience for the media covering its promotional events, especially sports reporters who covered the boxing matches and the auto races popular at that time. Boxing great Joe Louis was hired as a greeter at the hotel, patiently signing autographs for the tourists by the elevators for hours at a time. When Louis died in 1981, Caesars chairman Clifford Perlman made sure that Louis received a tribute befitting a champion and the hotel catered his funeral reception.

I came from a newspaper and wire service with strict guidelines against accepting gifts and favors from news sources, a practice which was largely ignored by sports and TV media. Thus, when I was told in my first week that Barbara Walters was coming to the Palace, be sure that she is met at the airport with a limousine and driver, my first thought was *why can't she take a cab like everyone else?* However, the limo was sent. Such a courtesy meant nothing to us and it paid off in good public and media relations.

I can honestly say that no one at Caesars ever asked me to do anything legally or morally wrong in my years heading their corporate public relations and shareholder relations program. In fact, it was the best job I ever had in terms of money and challenge. Reporters and editors spend their working lives as observers of the passing parade. It was fun to be on the inside of a corporation and have my views on many subjects respected.

I also would be untruthful if I didn't say that I got used to traveling in the corporate jet, having a limousine and driver at my disposal, and being greeted in each of the hotels by my colleagues who became friends. It was a convenient and interesting life even if we devoted seven days a week to it.

There is a hotel/casino culture referred to as "hotel groupies" who spend so much time on the property that they have no other life, an unhealthy situation. They work, they eat and drink at the hotels, and they have their romances. Windows are in short supply at the back of the house. Clocks don't exist in the casinos because they want the players to keep betting, unaware of the passage of time. A people mover transported folks from the sidewalk into the casino, not out. The oblivion to the outside world affects nearly every large hotel operation. The senior staff used to deliberately take walking breaks outside the hotel to know if the sun was shining. Also, most casinos have a regulatory rule against employees betting in the casino in off-hours so they won't, in effect, owe their soul to the company store if they lose.

During my years at Caesars, the corporation took advantage of New Jersey's decision to revitalize Atlantic City by permitting casino gambling, an experiment which has become common in the

United States and abroad as a tax revenue producer for governments and increased tourism. Gaming was approved by the New Jersey Legislature in a final effort to save a dying city which had been a popular resort in the early 20th century and before. One of the grandest hotels on the Boardwalk in its heyday was The Traymore. When the old hotel finally was demolished, the cost of the dynamite to do the job cost more than the value of the hotel. Most of the rest of the city could have been demolished, too, and it would have improved the Atlantic Ocean view.

The company purchased a rundown Howard Johnson motel on the Boardwalk and essentially rebuilt it. My colleague, Pete Summers, his public relations partner, Bill Coffin, and I shuttled back and forth dozens of times from Los Angeles to Atlantic City via Philadelphia as the work progressed on Caesars Boardwalk Regency (now called Caesars Atlantic City).

In fact, I obtained my Masters in Business Administration by doing my homework on those cross-country flights. I decided to get my MBA when my Caesars financial colleague, Duane Eberlein, told me that I needed a better grounding in business to work for a publicly-held company like Caesars.

The corporation would have paid the tuition, but I was so afraid that I might flunk that I paid it myself so I wouldn't be beholden to anyone. It was a foolish or unnecessary decision perhaps, but I don't regret it. The payoff for me, besides business knowledge, was being able later to command a higher salary as a teacher.

While the Boardwalk Regency was being revamped, the staff worked in trailers in a parking lot across the street from the hotel. One hot August afternoon, I emerged from one of the work trailers and was standing on the corner, thinking what to do or where to go next. As I stood blinking in the sunlight, a young black girl in a mini-skirt, high heels and heavy makeup sidled up to me. "Hey Whitey, you get off my corner. This is MY corner."

"Oh, I'm terribly sorry," I mumbled, moving off quickly. I should have been flattered that she considered me a threat to her profession.

J. Terrence Lanni headed the Atlantic City hotel rebuilding efforts during my tenure. In 2004, *Time* magazine said the veteran casino executive was known for his integrity and good name. Terry has the wonderful ability and memory to match names and faces. He engendered loyalty among the staff by being able to repeatedly call the newest busboy or janitor by the person's first name. I envied him the gift of remembrance and name association.

As anyone who opens a new building or operation knows, the minor problems can be as formidable as the major ones. The revamped hotel had only been open two weeks when a hotel plumber noticed water seeping under the public women's restroom on the lobby floor. He entered the facility to find the elegant gold sink fixtures had been removed, evidently taken as souvenirs.

There is a mentality that says the hotel/casino owes a customer for betting money there, but stealing is stealing no matter the circumstances. Take the soaps, the shampoos or the matches, that is expected, but don't complain when the room clock or radio is bolted to the table, the pictures on the walls are unmoveable, or you are charged for missing towels or blankets.

As anyone in retailing knows, people will swipe anything in a public place that isn't nailed down—and sometimes even if it is. There is a fair amount of larceny in most of us if we think we won't get caught.

When actor/director George Clooney announced in 2005 that he and a group of developers were planning on constructing a boutique hotel/casino off the Strip in Las Vegas, I smiled when he was quoted as saying, "We will have some sort of dress code, so that it will feel like you are walking into a more formal Las Vegas of a different age or a classic Monte Carlo casino" in Europe.

He said that his resort won't aim for the tank-top, shorts and sandals crowd that travel Las Vegas Boulevard to gape at the volcano, pirate ships, and animals at the commercial hotel/casinos. He was going for "class," he indicated.

I smiled because we tried to enforce a dress code at the Boardwalk Regency when it first opened, too, but the rules only lasted about a month. When the casino-operated tour buses arrived in the snow on Saturday night from New York and Philadelphia and hundreds of people piled off clutching their one-free-bet tickets, we knew we weren't going to be successful with our dress code program.

It was the year of the leisure suit for men—light green was favored—and the women wore chiffon cocktail dresses which smelled vaguely of mothballs, clutching their fake furs to keep warm. It simply wasn't feasible or practical to tell men to wear tuxedos or women to wear ball gowns, although it certainly looked nicer in the formal dining rooms or at the shows. Clooney said it was "a romantic notion" and it was. Perhaps it will be more successful in the desert.

One gambling myth to debunk, however, is that the house never loses. I was at Caesars Palace in Las Vegas one night when a Chinese high roller from Hong Kong arrived about midnight with four suitcases full of cash. He played Baccarat, a high stakes card game, all night.

The major talk at the staff breakfast the next morning was how he had taken the house for more than a million dollars. It does happen and the casino is well aware of it. It's strictly a money business. The trick for the casinos is to make the playing and the ambience so attractive that players will remain at the tables or slot machines until their wins become losses.

For the uninitiated, a "high roller" refers to a customer with a good credit rating and probably a high-level account at the hotel who receives *gratis* a room/suite, food and beverages of his choice (known as RFB). If the guest is comfortable, he or she will continue to bet, spend money in the luxurious shops and entertainment venues, and return again for the royal treatment at his favorite hotel/casino. It is a smart marketing ploy that has paid off handsomely for Las Vegas, Atlantic City, and Lake Tahoe and is spreading worldwide.

Twenty-five years ago, it was considered by the gaming companies to be a huge financial risk to build a hotel/casino for $100 million. Steve Wynn's 50-story Wynn Las Vegas was built in 2005 for an estimated $2.7 billion—and the crowds keep coming.

As a sidelight, carpeting under the casino gaming tables must be replaced often because a serious male player won't take a bathroom break. With thousands of dollars at stake, it is easier to relieve himself on the floor while he sits at the tables. Women don't have that luxury.

I also was surprised when I first went to the hotels that movie, TV, and sports personalities frequently were paged repeatedly by the hotel switchboard in public rooms and at poolside. When I questioned the fact that I knew a certain movie personality wasn't in the hotel, I was told by a press agent that it was the cheapest form of publicity available and it added to the aura of excitement that a famous person might be in the hotel, or headed there. The tourists loved it…and all it took was one phone call.

I was supported in my public relations efforts by my colleague Pete Summers, a raconteur and public relations man of the old school where image and personal contacts were paramount. A tall, white-haired gentleman who was handsome enough to have been hired occasionally to film television commercials, Pete moved to California in the '70s to play golf and escape the eastern winters.

He was a partner in the public relations firm that worked for Caesars properties as an outside-the-company supplementary source for me and for the hotels. We also produced the company's annual and quarterly reports from my office. A generous man who lived well on his client expense accounts, Pete never traveled by car or cab when a limousine and driver were available. He died broke, but he had a lot of fun in the process.

We had many adventures.

One night we flew to Philadelphia from Los Angeles, rented a car at the airport and drove to downtown Philadelphia to stay at the old Bellevue-Stratford Hotel. There was a heavy rainstorm the next morning and we were going to New York by train. The rental car company said they were unable to claim the car at the hotel, and I didn't have the time or the inclination to return it to the airport in the rain.

I appealed to Pete who was rightfully called "Bullshit Pete" by the Caesars executive staff. He called the rental car company from his room.

"This is Mr. Summers from Caesars World Corporation and I have a small problem," he said in his deep voice. "One of your cars was assigned to Miss Kilgore last night and it is here at the hotel. Unfortunately, Miss Kilgore passed away last night and I am so busy making funeral arrangements that I don't have time to return the car. I'm sure you understand." I collapsed laughing on the hotel room floor.

"That's terrible," said the woman on the other end of the line. "Was it sudden?"

"Just like THAT," Pete continued, snapping his fingers for emphasis.

"We'll send someone right over," the woman said. "Just leave the keys at the desk."

We hailed a cab and left immediately for the train station.

Pete was in partnership in a New York public relations firm for many years, proud that he had represented United Technologies in their early growth years. He always said that his contribution to the firm was to bring people together and be the troubleshooter. He didn't bother with the nitty-gritty details, although he could write a press release, if necessary.

In my office one day, Pete said he wanted to take his wife Barbara and a couple of friends to dinner on Saturday night at Morton's restaurant in Beverly Hills. In the early days, the restaurant was so snooty that they had an unlisted telephone number. Only the Hollywood elite need apply. I had acquired the phone number and Pete used my office phone to call for four reservations.

"Do we know you?" The restaurant voice asked him.

"Well, 90 percent of the people DO," he bluffed indignantly. He got the reservations.

One time, a young man on the corporate team—who had been fired for incompetence—came into my office to say goodbye. I expressed my regrets that he was leaving. Instead of commenting further, he stopped me cold by saying, "If you send my headshot photo to the newspaper, will you please be sure that it shows my good side with my smile and dimples showing? I want to be sure I look good." I hope he got another job.

Because I was on the corporate side, I had only limited dealings with the entertainment personalities who performed at the hotels. As a hotel executive said bitterly to me once "We make the money, corporate spends it." As the older stars are dying or retiring, it has become increasingly difficult to find personalities who can fill a showroom, especially one with wide universal appeal to middle America. Most of the personalities under contract to Caesars, like the actress/singer Ann-Margret and yes, Frank Sinatra, were businesslike in their dealings and generally fulfilled the terms of their contracts. Ann-Margret was a special favorite in Atlantic City because all she ever required was transportation to get there and home and the audiences loved her.

It is generally known and accepted by the media that if you want to make contact with a corporate executive or ask for a favor, the public relations personnel are the people to see. Public relations people are hired to put the best face on a company crisis, produce the public material and advertising, and generally tread a fine line between serving the company and the public in all its forms.

As a slang description, probably from the military, public relations people often are referred to as "flacks" because they deflect the bad news or flack and accentuate the positive. That's what they are paid to do.

Thus, it never occurred to me to say no when the president of UPI called me at my office in late afternoon, the day before New Year's Eve. Through our long association, I remained friendly with all of them.

We chatted for a few minutes and then he got to the point of his call from his home in Connecticut. Could I book him a suite at Caesars Palace for a party of four for New Year's Eve?

He and his wife and another couple planned to fly to Las Vegas the next day to celebrate the new year. He sounded all right on the phone, although it did go through my mind that he and his companions might be having a few drinks and decided a trip West would be nice. I knew that the Palace was booked solid for the holidays, but I said I would call and ask them.

I didn't bother with the reservations system. I called the general manager of the hotel on our direct line and told him my problem. Not surprisingly, he said there's no room at the inn.

"But this is the head of a major wire service," I whined. "You've got to find him something."

An hour later, he called me back, told me that he had pulled the reservation of a well-known movie personality, and the UPI executive could have the suite.

"You owe me dinner," he said, laughing. I agreed that I did. I called the president and gave him the directions and confirmation. Then I went home for the holiday.

Two days later, the Palace manager called me, furious. The expected party didn't show, didn't call, and the hotel lost the revenue on New Year's Eve from a $1,000-a-night suite which stood empty. I was upset, the manager was upset, and no one answered the home phone when I called Connecticut for an explanation. I honestly feared for my job because everyone in the company seemed to know that I had gone out on a limb for these no-shows.

The UPI chief infuriated me even more when I saw him at a journalism gathering several months later. He seemed indifferent to what he had done or hadn't done.

"We had a few drinks and going to Las Vegas for New Years seemed like a good idea at the time," he said, as I stalked away. No apology was ever forthcoming.

As the song says, whatever happened to class?

Settling into a desk job in the '90s.

10

LOS ANGELES
Teaching and Streaking

I was teaching part-time at Los Angeles Trade-Technical College, an inner city community college where students go to obtain enough credits to transfer to the state university system by studying liberal arts subjects, or learn useful trades to help them make a living. I have the utmost respect for these college students who are trying to better themselves and make a contribution to their families and communities, most of them working full-time while going to school.

Part-timers like me were known as "Freeway Flyers" because that's where we spent too much time—on Los Angeles freeways —while shuttling between classrooms. I taught in the communi- ty college system for nearly 15 years while working at full-time jobs because I felt it was important and I liked the interaction with the students. I learned more from them than they did from me, I'm sure, in terms of different cultures and the way they viewed the world.

Trade-Tech was a "cement school" on the edge of the crime- ridden downtown, although the gardeners tried hard to make grass and roses grow in the shadow of the brick and adobe build- ings to give it a campus feeling. Teachers were advised for their own safety never to be alone in remote areas or top floors of the buildings, especially teaching night classes. Room doors and faculty bathrooms were locked, and everyone learned how to reach police security quickly.

It wasn't the students who were the problem, but street people who wandered into classrooms or hallways to camp for the night or, as happened on occasional Saturdays, to streak naked through the halls to cause a sensation. Usually, no one gave them a second glance.

Essentially, though, faculty and students looked out for each other. Graduations were nice events when families excitedly joined together perhaps to see the only member of their family graduate from a school, and sports and social events were encouraged. At graduation, students wore caps and gowns and everyone dressed up.

One night I received a call at home from a lawyer who said he represented one of my students. He said the young man had been picked up on a repeat traffic violation and was serving 30 days in county jail. The lawyer said that with time on his hands in incarceration, his client was concerned that he would fall behind in his school work and could I possibly give him some homework assignments? I was glad to help and the lawyer sent an aide to my classroom to pick up the work. I am proud to say that the young man returned to class eventually with all of his homework completed, he graduated, and went on to the Cal State University system. I learned later that he, too, had become a teacher.

While I was teaching, I also left Caesars World in a management change. It was fortuitous in its way because Mother suffered a series of heart attacks while she was spending the winter in California with my sister's family and with me. She was in and out of the hospital for several weeks recuperating at my place and I was available to care for her. When she was finally well enough, I took her home to Westfield and then flew back to Los Angeles for a month-long vacation in Spain, Morocco, and Portugal.

In the Fall, I heard that Ernst & Whinney, one of the Big Eight accounting firms when there still were such entities, was seeking to hire a West Coast public relations person because the city had received the bid to stage the 1984 Summer Olympics and E&W was designated to do the official scorekeeping. The scores were to be done by computer for the first time.

A couple of my colleagues who had been at Caesars World suggested that I apply for the job along with Duane (my friend from the accounting department who had originally told me to apply for my MBA to gain more business experience). He applied at E&W as a certified public accountant. Duane and I were both hired at E&W (now Ernst & Young), and although we didn't entirely regret the move, we didn't find it much fun or challenging after the years at Caesars.

Certified public accountant education and training is as rigorous as it is for lawyers, but they tend to be a different breed of cats. Accountants often are introverts, comfortable with figures more than people, and critical of anyone who doesn't meet their exacting standards. Also, they often are workaholics and not team players, which was hard for me to recognize coming from journalism where you hang together or you hang alone.

Management was aware of this mindset and hired a full-time psychological counselor at the Cleveland, Ohio, headquarters who spent his time dealing with drug, alcohol, and marital problems among the partners who had trouble relating to every day conflicts. He told me that many marriages were in a shambles because the husband was super-critical of wives and children who didn't toe the line as the accountants were trained to do.

Duane and I decided early on that we weren't hired for our

skills, but rather because E&W was anxious to obtain Caesars World as an accounting client and apparently they thought we could provide entree to the company. This theory was borne out when we were asked to write detailed memos about the workings and personalities of Caesars management, which we refused to do. We saw no reason to burn our bridges with our former employers and friends. We didn't openly fight the request, we just ignored it. And like many issues in large corporations, it went away.

I always enjoyed the story about rival accounting firm, Price Waterhouse, who represented the legendary movie producer Alfred Hitchcock in his business dealings. When Hitchcock died, the firm sent flowers to his funeral and then billed the estate.

E&W represented talk show host Johnny Carson in his enterprises and had a room for accountants set aside in the Century City office—known as "the Carson room"—where his businesses were handled exclusively.

The summer Olympics were exciting to be part of, although it wasn't easy to sell our scorekeeping to the media as a fascinating story. Even the firm chairman came out from Cleveland to receive a formal presentation from the staff on how they were going to computerize the scoring. After listening for nearly an hour, he said, "Is that all there is?" And he went to lunch.

I called the bureau chief at *Business Week* one day to pitch the computer story to him for an Olympic segment they were publishing. After I burbled on for several minutes and told him we would be happy to give him a computer demonstration, he started to laugh.

"Maggie, that's the most boring story I ever heard," said he. "So, you've got computers adding up scores. So what?" Secretly, I had to laugh, too, because computers were still developing in the marketplace. Eventually, *Business Week* did do a story on the scorekeeping, but he let me twist slowly in the wind for awhile.

Under businessman Peter Uebberoth's direction, the Olympic committee wisely invested the money which was donated to them and it became a money-making proposition, a model for future Olympic venues.

My friend Jack Brannan and I attended most of the Olympic events, which were so well run by hundreds of volunteers that it enhanced Los Angeles' reputation as a significant city under Mayor Tom Bradley. He said it was the highlight of his career. A year later, I was asked to attend a reunion party of Olympic participants, but I had a scheduling conflict and couldn't be there. The reunion never happened because people had scattered by then...and the party was over.

The best thing about the years at E&W were the friendships I made with Nancy, one of the few women CPAs at the firm, and with Guy, my counterpart nationally, in Cleveland. They like to travel, as I do, and we have made the scene in Australia, Hong Kong, Bangkok, and other Far East exotic spots in recent years.

After the Olympics were over, E&W had no further need for public relations and they subsequently merged with Arthur Young, another large accounting firm. I decided to go on my own for a change and formed my own public relations and writing firm for a decade. As one of my potential clients said once, plaintively, "We are the best kept secret in Southern California. Can you help us raise our image?" I could and I did.

Also in the '80s when Ronald Reagan was in the White House, the press corps spent most major holidays either in Santa Barbara when he and Nancy were at their ranch or in Palm Springs for New Years when they joined their California friends for an annual reunion. Because Helen Thomas, still with UPI, doesn't drive, I was her chauffeur and companion on these trips and visited with old friends.

We had a good time, but if anything serious had happened to the president, the press corps probably would have been the last to know. His mountaintop ranch was about 30 miles away from the press motel in Santa Barbara and quite inaccessible on narrow roads, although we made driving forays up there.

The only glimpse we got of him was when he rode horseback and that was filtered through the photographers' long distance lenses. Reagan liked to joke that if he really wanted to scare the press corps when he went horseback riding, he had only to clutch his chest to simulate a heart attack, and the group would go wild.

In Palm Springs, he and the first lady stayed at the 100-acre estate of publisher Walter Annenberg and his wife, Leonore, who was Reagan's chief of protocol. The couple also served in London when Annenberg was U.S. Ambassador to the Court of St. James.

The estate was surrounded by a high wall and the closest any media got to the guests was standing outside at the intersection of Frank Sinatra Drive and Bob Hope Boulevard, like hungry orphans with their noses pressed to the glass of a warm bakery.

It was undignified, but the media bosses back on the East Coast felt it was necessary to pay to have staff on the scene in case some of the VIPs made news. At least Palm Springs and Santa Barbara was more luxurious than Plains, Georgia with Jimmy Carter or Crawford, Texas with George W. Bush.

As I have traveled with Helen over the years, I have always been fascinated by total strangers who seek her out for autographs or to shake her hand. She is unfailingly gracious—as are other members of the celebrity White House press corps—but it was not unusual when the group was in Santa Barbara for well-dressed strangers to appear in the press room, sit down like they belonged there, and want to talk politics even with the fellows who had a card game underway.

Often, these local residents would hang around until someone invited them for a meal or permitted them to sit through a press briefing. Santa Barbara may not be the most exciting city in America, but "get a life" comes to mind to explain their actions.

During those years, Helen and I also had long, informative dinners with our friends, Abigail Van Buren (Dear Abby), the advice columnist, and her kind husband Morton Phillips. The conversation was always stimulating and we laughed a lot. Abby's advice was to enjoy life because this is no dress rehearsal for the real thing.

I am indebted to the actress, June Lockhart, for the following story which I thought was cute.

June, a friend of many in the media, played the mother on the old *Lassie* television shows and is a member of an acting family. It wasn't generally known, but Lassie (there were several) was a male because they are said to be easier to train. Rudd Weatherwax, a professional movie animal trainer, always insisted that the members of the *Lassie* cast come out to his ranch in the San Fernando Valley, near Hollywood, to meet with the dog and to develop a rapport. If Lassie didn't like the person, the cast member was dropped from the show. Very tough to depend on a dog for a job.

Word went out that the show was looking for an actor to play a forest ranger, a good part. Several actors made the trek to the ranch, only to be rejected because the dog appeared not to like them.

Finally, a male actor who really needed the work heard about the dog's likes and dislikes. He developed a plan. The actor borrowed a bitch-in-heat from a friend one day and played with the dog all afternoon. He had her dog hair all over his clothes, her saliva, her "smell." Then he went to the ranch. Well, the male Lassie went crazy...couldn't stay away from the actor. Very affectionate.

The fellow got the job.

A Hindu wedding on Bali, Indonesia, July 2000.
The bride's crown weighed 10 pounds.

11

ASIA
Promoting Excellence in Journalism

A s the new century loomed, I decided to reevaluate my life and if traveling was what I wanted to do, I'd better do it. I was approaching retirement age and my finances were limited because my long career at UPI yielded only a small pension—the price of a couple of lunches at my favorite bistros.

The money was paid by the federal Pension Benefit Corporation established by Congress in the 1970s to provide pension guarantees to employees such as UPI workers who had seen the retirement money reduced when UPI struggled through two bankruptcies. As the PBC said in their approval letter: "We will pay you a certain amount every month. And when you die, that is the end." Duh!

As always, when I needed help I put out the word to my Washington friends. They have never failed me. I sent an e-mail to my dear friend Bill Eaton, who was heading a program for foreign exchange students at the University of Maryland. I told him that I was looking for a foreign teaching program that would pay me to travel, perhaps work with young journalists in emerging democracies, and give something back to the profession.

I was not a novice teacher. I taught part-time at universities and community colleges in Los Angeles for 15 years while also working in journalism and public relations, teaching business subjects to inner city college students who often didn't even know how to write a check.

Bill replied immediately with "Have I got a job for you!" And indeed he did. I applied for the Knight Foundation International Press Fellowship administered by the International Center for Journalists (ICFJ) in Washington. It was my second fellowship because I had already received the Ford Foundation Fellowship when I worked on the *Los Angeles Times*.

I requested Asia since I was most familiar with the area and because I am not bilingual it would be possible to teach in English there. It is one thing to speak tourist or "kitchen" French or Spanish, but much more difficult to stand in front of a classroom to teach in a foreign language even with a translator by your side.

Nine of us were accepted into the Knight program, established by the publisher John S. Knight and his brother James in 1993 to promote excellence in journalism and press freedom worldwide. There were more than 200 applicants for the Spring 2000 program for mid-career journalists. I was long past mid-career, but who's counting?

I went to Washington for a week of orientation at the ICFJ center near the White House. My only real recollection of the training week was the warning that if the country we were visiting had political turmoil, don't get involved and don't pitch in to help in the newsroom. You are there as a guest of the country and stop thinking like a working journalist.

During the four months in Southeast Asia, I visited, trained, and advised journalists and students in 10 countries including Nepal, Bangladesh, Thailand, Singapore, Calcutta, Hong Kong, Malaysia, and Indonesia. I also returned to my old stomping grounds in

Vietnam and Cambodia.

Since modesty is the watchword even in liberal Muslim countries, I ordered three inexpensive ankle-length skirts from Sears Roebuck with matching tops to cover my arms. Occasionally I wore a head scarf. Even then men on the street, especially in Malaysia, stared at the nail polish on my toes and fingers. I avoided shorts except at the swimming pool. No sense in insulting my hosts.

I left Los Angeles for Singapore on April 1, 2000 with a two-day stopover in Honolulu to visit friends. I arrived in Singapore after midnight, and after clearing customs went directly by cab to the Singapore Marriott hotel on fashionable Orchard Road. It was so late they had given my reservation away, forcing me into a three-room suite at the same price, larger than my apartment.

When I roused myself several hours later, I called my Los Angeles friend, Carol Scott, who headed Asian public relations for the oil company Unocal. She worked in the Far East for nearly a dozen years for them in Bangkok and Singapore. Carol, who had a car, picked me up at the hotel for lunch and we drove to her black and white villa on the edge of the city. Her maid, Maravic, met me along with Carol's wonderful French poodle, Bella.

Maravic, a Filipina, served tea in Carol's living room while we traded stateside news. Maravic was one of thousands of Asians who work as domestics in other countries for years at a time because their home country can't provide enough jobs to support them. She had a husband in Manila and a child named Waylon Boy being raised by her parents.

Maravic, a tall, attractive, intelligent woman in her 30s, sent nearly every cent she made home to the family, and Carol paid her way home for Christmas and vacations. On their days off every Sunday, the maids would gather in churchyards or other public places to share their mail from home, probably gossip about their employers, and eat potluck meals of their native dishes.

I stayed with Carol for a month at the villa—left over from British colonial days, with two broad balconies on each level of the house facing out on a broad expanse of green lawn and palm trees to the Singapore (MRT) tracks beyond.

There are several amusing versions of a story about the building of Singapore's clean, modern subway system in the 1980s. They were very proud of this engineering feat, and with good reason since Singapore rose from lowlands and swamp. At the ribbon-cutting ceremony on opening day, dignitaries from the surrounding region were invited to a gala celebration. Everyone was in place for a ride when to their chagrin, the subway cars wouldn't open. After a quick inspection, it was determined that someone had stuck a wad of chewing gum in one of the doors, shorting out the system.

As former Prime Minister Lee Kwan Yew said in his memoirs in 2000, he was so infuriated by the incident that he decided his people weren't ready—or didn't deserve—a clean, efficient mass transit system. He had earlier banned the sale of chewing gum in Singapore and there was a hefty fine for littering. Lee decided that Singaporeans were irresponsible in disposing of the sticky stuff and he wanted a clean republic. The gum ban was modified in 2004, but chewing gum is still frowned on there and it is difficult to obtain.

When I traveled by bus and train to Malacca and Kuala Lumpur in Malaysia, the bus made a rest stop after the border crossing. Passengers piled off the bus, rushed into the station, and returned with armloads of gum by the carton, chewing all the way.

When I recovered from jet lag, I called my ICFJ contact, Vijay Menon, director of the Asian Media Information and Communication Center (AMIC), where Menon rented space for

$2 a year at Nanyang University, about 18 miles outside Singapore near Jurong Point, reached by a combination of subway and campus bus or more directly by taxi. Because we didn't know each other, Menon and I agreed to meet the next day at the main library in downtown Singapore and drove to rather spacious quarters on the campus where he maintained a staff of 25 young Asians and westerners who wrote reports on the progress of journalism in Asia and set up conferences to talk about it.

There are numerous radio, television and newspaper groups all over Asia, many designed to challenge freedom of the press restrictions in countries that give press freedom only lip service and other groups designed merely for sociability.

I was assigned an office with a computer, telephone and mail service at AMIC, my base for the next four months. Vijay, a tall middle-aged Indian with a nice sense of humor, told me my first mission was to go to Nepal and work with young business writers. I had been to Nepal several times during the Vietnam years and I was delighted. As the weeks went on, Vijay and I established an informal relationship where he would use his many contacts to set up classes, forums, symposiums, media meetings and interviews for me to join in each country. Because he had a competent network of in-country professionals in the places that I visited, I was provided with dates, locations, advance publicity and on-site help to conduct, workshops, make speeches or simply have dinner with Asian acquaintances.

I would return from a country, like Nepal, and he would hand me a list of media contacts in another country who might want to meet with me. If I approved, I would go to the country for a few weeks at a time and then return to Singapore for another assignment. I worked hard, but the program worked well. After all, young journalists in emerging democracies were being given an opportunity to meet with a western woman journalist and it was free to them because my fellowship paid for it. What's not to like?

The only country I skipped in the region was Sri Lanka, which has been in political upheaval for so many years that freedom of the press is a myth. (I hear they have great beaches, however).

Unfortunately, my trip to Nepal was delayed nearly a month because I was quite incapacitated with an attack of cellulitis—a bacterial infection exacerbated by heat and humidity that made walking difficult and wearing shoes impossible. I stayed in bed at Carol's most of the time until she finally forced me to go to a Chinese doctor recommended by the U.S. Embassy when she noted that medical treatment in Nepal would be difficult to obtain and the disease was worsening. Bella rarely left my bedside, mostly because I had air conditioning in my room and a supply of cookies to share.

I finally left for Kathmandu on April 23, Easter Sunday. Nepal is a little landlocked country (many jokes about the Nepalese Navy) with India on their southern border and Tibet/China to the north. The country has tried democracy for several decades with mixed success.

Since my visit, the popular king and his family were assassinated at a family gathering by a drug-crazed son and there were numerous Maoist battles as the Chinese threatened to take over the country. In February 2005, King Gyanendra declared a state of emergency that caused a series of violent demonstrations as protesters demanded the restoration of democracy in the Himalayan kingdom.

As much as I like Nepal and its people, I was disappointed at their lack of progress, although the political upheaval slowed them down. The nation's economy depends heavily on the mountain climbers who visit Mount Everest, the world's highest mountain, on the Nepal-Tibet border, and pay the government for the privilege of trying to scale it.

The taxi driver en route from shabby Kathmandu Airport to the comfortable Himalaya Hotel pointed with pride to a new sports stadium that was rarely used while the streets were unpaved and the locals couldn't drink the water without boiling it. In the immediate countryside, there were small brick homes and apartments being built, many for the local politicians.

As arranged by AMIC, I took a taxi the first day to the Nepal Press Institute in the heart of the city, down a dirt lane and up five flights of a walkup in a building where media classes were conducted, training was held, and there was equipment for computer and TV programming with much of the money provided by charitable grants and loans from Europe, Australia, and the United States.

My hostess was Mrs. Beena Pradhan, undersecretary of the Ministry of Information and Communications, who was as uncertain as I who would show up for five days of business journalism workshops which included lunch. My experience in most of these emerging democracy countries was that editors, reporters, and photographers would attend if the sponsoring group was picking up the tab and reimbursing the journalists for their lost salaries. Their publications, by and large, don't pay well, many not at all.

Therefore, it is naive to expect a journalist to work only for one publication or broadcast outlet with total loyalty. Often, they work for several publications or moonlight for the government to put food on their tables. They don't view it as an ethical issue and they don't understand why westerners do. For them, it is simply a matter of Third World economics.

To Beena's and my surprise, 25 Nepalese male journalists did show up at the press institute, most stayed during the entire workshop and we got to know each other at frequent tea breaks. The reporters were all young men although they do have women reporters on their three major newspapers that publish daily in English, Nepali, and Kantipur. I was pleased to be asked to return to Nepal in September to speak to women magazine reporters and editors, but by then my fellowship had ended. Monsoons closed the airport in July and August.

There were assorted magazines and other publications plus government-run television and radio stations. The *Kathmandu Post* built a $70 million newspaper plant with the latest in computer and printing equipment, but with only a 30 percent literacy rate in a population of 25 million people and one television set per 1,000 people, the best way to reach the populace, in Nepal and elsewhere, is by radio.

Bharat Koirala, who headed the institute and was an educated, traveled man, was justifiably proud of his local radio operation where he went into villages, taught them to set up broadcast facilities which provided needed health information, for example, such as birth control or AIDS advisories. He also posted information on village walls and trees in Nepali to reach those who could read.

My efforts at the journalism workshop in Nepal and elsewhere were supplemented by college professors, local economists or an occasional local senior journalist. It helped me to fill the time and also supplement my remarks. It also helped the reporters with local contacts they could use in the future and it meant that they didn't have to concentrate on understanding my English when a native speaker was available.

I rarely used a full-time translator because most educated Asians understand and read English even if they are too shy to speak it. If I needed a translator, someone in the group could help. You simply aren't communicating if you haven't sat through a two-hour lecture on economic policy delivered in Nepali, but I felt it was important for the journalists to understand him than to bother with translation so I could understand. The press institutes chose the supplemental speakers, often from the local university, wherever I went and they graciously accepted.

I recall writing a letter to my sister in Stockton, California, while an economist droned on in his language in a hot, crowded little classroom with undersized school room chairs with arm rests for note-taking.

Bugs and birds flew in and and out the open windows while traffic and animals moved on the streets below. Large brown monkeys sat in the trees along major streets waiting to pounce on unsuspecting shoppers carrying fruit and vegetables in their string shopping bags. The animals were harmless, but unnerving.

I showed video training tapes while we discussed freedom of access to information, ethics in journalism, and general reporting. To show that they were part of the electronic age, the students jeered loudly when a young reporter wrote his story on an old manual typewriter in the videotape. They thought it was even funnier when I told them I had begun my career using a typewriter. Asians generally are very hip to computers and they watch the international editions of CNN and the BBC via satellite.

It seems that all young Nepalese reporters dream about becoming wire service reporters or stringers (part-timers) for major publications outside the country, although their major gripe about sources was how uncooperative private companies and their public relations people were in refusing to talk to them in Kathmandu.

A writer for the *London Times*, who dropped by to help me, told these kids to stop complaining, get out and meet some of the corporate people, American and European, who have offices in the country.

"Don't be lazy," he said. "You are invited to embassy parties and company functions and you should go. Why should their public relations people talk to you if they don't know you?"

The thought seemed to sink in.

The press institute told newspapers and TV that they should set up specific beats for their reporters to cover tourism, environmental and medical issues, entertainment and religion, but the trained manpower isn't available. The reporters who do work for the media are reasonably well-educated, but most only attend junior college and trade schools. Compulsory education only extends from ages 6 to 11. It is a country of Muslims, Buddhists, and Hindus.

However, I have the utmost respect for a reporter or editor who can cover a story in his own language and translate it to English, all while working against a print or broadcast deadline. I couldn't do it and I don't know many western reporters who could. As part of my efforts, I met with many reporters over tea at my hotel. I also was interviewed by assorted media—a few in English—about why I liked Nepal. (Let me count the reasons.)

In my travels, I also made it a point to meet with any women journalists who cared to meet with me. It often was a gripe session on their part because they frequently were overlooked and under-paid, but I hope it encouraged them to meet with another woman writer who understood their goals and aspirations.

On a visit to the *Kathmandu Post*, I encountered a reporter sitting at his computer with a syndicated copy of a crossword puzzle on his lap which he was translating from English into Nepali for the Sunday paper. I asked what he did when the letters didn't fit.

"They always fit," he replied, "because if they don't, I just make up something. And I don't work Mondays, so I don't have to answer the angry reader phone calls."

In my off-hours in Kathmandu, I visited a government-sponsored craft fair, toured Durbar Square (the historic seat of royalty), returned to the still-beautiful Yak and Yeti Hotel where the silverware was still greasy and the waiters still surly.

I hired a car and driver one afternoon that unexpectedly took me to a cremation site in a nearby town where the men, in white shirts and dark trousers, sat smoking and talking in small groups on the rocks waiting for their turn to "burn Grandma." The deceased was wrapped mummy-style in yellow cheese cloth, placed on a pyre of wood and hot coals, burned for four to six hours, prayers said, and the remains dropped into the filthiest stream I ever encountered where the locals also bathed. Large monkeys cavorted among the rocks and trees while the cremation was proceeding. It was late in the afternoon, raining and dark...a scene I will never forget.

I also visited the National Museum on the edge of town, a modest villa with displays of ancient tools and weapons used by these once-tribal people. I always spend time in all the countries I visit to tour the national museums because I gain a sense of history and perspective from the experience.

As I rounded a corner in the building, I was delighted to see a hand-lettered white sign in English that said: "We wish to thank the people of Los Angeles, California, for returning our stolen artifacts." There were a few clay pots and a statue or two on the shelf.

Since artifact looting is a major problem in older countries and I live in Los Angeles, I was proud to see the sign. However, one of my less reverent friends observed that one of the Los Angeles museums simply may have been returning what they swiped in the first place.

Who knows?

Observation One: Some countries, like some family members, always need help.

Observation Two: The poorer the nation, the more gracious the people.

That was my experience in Dhaka, Bangladesh (Dacca-English spelling) where overcrowding and poverty are immense obstacles to development; where the average annual income is $350 a year for a population of 130 million people; and a literacy rate of only 40 percent even with free, compulsory education.

Dhaka potentially is a nice city with wide boulevards and parks, a good university in the city center with attractive red stone buildings and a broad campus, and an emerging middle class. But as people pour in from the countryside to seek jobs and street begging is a way of life, it is difficult to see a successful future for this small country of 56,000 square miles (about the size of Iowa), much of it built on low tropical marshland that is among the rainiest in the world. Bangladesh makes world headlines annually when flooding causes havoc and boats capsize drowning thousands of natives.

My host, Professor Q.A.I.M. Nuruddin of the journalism department at the University of Dhaka, said, "When I arrived here in the 1950s, Dhaka was a nice little town of 10,000 people. The people started arriving from the interior seeking jobs and the city is now trying to accommodate 10 million people."

A UNICEF representative said she thought they were getting a handle on overpopulation, but no one really believes it. The port terminal was crowded with families living and cooking on its stone floors. City Council passed an ordinance stating that new buildings could only be painted white or the stucco left untouched, which only adds to its bleakness.

The British controlled the area that became Bangladesh from the 18th century until 1947 when East Bengal became part of Pakistan. Since then, governments have come and gone with considerable turmoil and corruption until an Islamic republic was declared in 1988. The official language is Bangla, but the educated people speak some English. The young journalists watch international television and they want quick success.

A strict Muslim and Hindu country, reporters are limited in their coverage and interpretations by an official secrecies act and a movie censorship board in this parliamentary democracy.

I was met at the airport by Professor Nuruddin and a small group of his colleagues who presented me with a bouquet of gladioli. I joked that I felt like a movie star. Actually, I was glad that the men met me because when we stepped outside the airport we were surrounded by filthy beggars who wanted to touch me and my belongings—and ask for money, of course. I had compassion for them, but I wanted them out of my space, too.

Our group immediately left for a meeting at my hotel to plan the week's work. I conducted a three-day workshop on business and financial reporting with about a dozen reporters in attendance. Because they were working journalists who would lose salary if they attended, the Press Institute of Bangladesh paid them 200 takas a day (about $10 U.S.) to attend plus lunch. I was amused that the attendees knew who Alan Greenspan, then Chairman of our Federal Reserve, was—my students in Los Angeles missed the question on three exams.

I was greatly aided at the workshops by Shahiduzzaman Khan, executive editor and news editor of *The Financial Express of Dhaka*, who helped with the translation and gave his local insights to the attending media, most with four or five years experience. Mr. Khan has close ties to the United States. His adult children live in Oklahoma and his wife, Sayeda, has written 12 books. I was honored to dine at their home.

Professor Nuruddin, who described himself as a "liberal" member of the five-member movie censorship board, said he took the position that "if the movie isn't fit for my wife, my mother, and my daughter to see, I vote against it." Nuruddin did graduate work at Southern Illinois University. He and Madame Nuruddin entertained me at an elegant dinner party in Dhaka with other faculty members and press institute leaders. I have high praise for UNICEF and UNESCO workers in the emerging democracy countries where they work very hard to make a difference in local lives.

One of the brighter and funnier men in Dhaka in 2000 was Harvard-educated M. Sakmal Husain, Secretary of Information, who spoke to one of my journalism workshops. President Bill Clinton had just made an 11-hour stop in Bangladesh on an Asian trip. I asked Husain if the trip was successful from his standpoint.

"It nearly put me in the hospital from nervous exhaustion," he laughed. "Just dealing with the U.S. Secret Service was a nightmare. We did everything they asked in terms of security, but it still wasn't enough. I know this is a common complaint from other host countries, but 11 hours seemed like 11 weeks until they left."

The local opposition newspaper noted "Clinton was here for 11 hours...and he didn't even leave us any money." They were pleased to be recognized as a country, however.

Japan, the Philippines, India, and Thailand are considered to be the only countries in Asia to have genuine freedom of the press, or more specifically, freedom of access to information , according to the United Nations Economic, Social and Cultural Organization (UNESCO), and even the Thailand government puts press freedom on a sliding scale of effectiveness.

The underlying problem in most of the emerging democratic countries is that freedom guarantees were not written in detail into the revised Constitutions of the countries involved, so the courts, the Parliaments, and the bureaucracy can play fast-and-loose with their interpretation of freedom. The recent rise of terrorism around the world has made press freedoms even more difficult to maintain and the struggle likely will continue.

After Bangladesh, I attended a journalism conference in wonderful Bangkok before heading for Calcutta, India. It is hard to think of Calcutta as The City of Joy. It isn't. Mother Theresa, their most famous citizen and an Albanian girl, had her work cut out for her when she went there, but even her lifelong efforts scarcely made a dent in the squalor, filth, and poverty. Plaster statues of the late nun in her blue and white habit were available for sale everywhere for only a few cents.

When I remarked to a friend that even Saigon during the war was better than Calcutta, she replied, "I've spent time in both places, too, and Saigon was nice by comparison." To be fair, India has made great strides in improvement in the last decade. *The Times of India* is on a par with the best of the world's newspapers and the business journalists, men and women, in Calcutta were well-educated and well-trained for the most part.

But the whole Calcutta visit was summed up for me when I got to the airport near midnight to leave for Hong Kong, the temperature was in the 90s, and there was only one potable (safe to drink) water fountain available. I stood in a long line waiting to drink at the fountain. The fellow ahead of me in line vomited his dinner in the fountain basin, then walked away.

I, too, walked away.

I also spent about a week in Kuala Lumpur, Malaysia, one of the more liberal Muslim countries, where I spoke to graduate and undergraduate journalism students and faculty at the University of Putra Malaysia on the edge of the city.

I spoke in a large, modern auditorium on campus on the opportunities in journalism today, including advertising, public relations, newspapers, magazines, television and online. I was standing at the onstage podium about three minutes into the speech, when the lights went out, a common occurrence in

Southeast Asia. I fumbled in my purse, found a flashlight, turned it on and continued speaking. The audience sat in darkness. About 10 minutes later, the auditorium lights came on again and everyone applauded. We had become comrades in adversity by then.

Many of the student questions centered on why Asia wasn't covered accurately or fairly by the western news media. They think they are victims of bad public relations. I heard similar complaints in other countries.

Having been a member of the western media in Asia once, I defended my colleagues, pointing out that they are often working under difficult deadlines in many languages in many different countries. Television, especially, often sends reporters to the story with very little background and information on a hit-or-miss basis. It is no secret that TV isn't interested if there isn't a photo-op. Certainly the Asians got immense coverage on the 2004/05 tsunami.

Whether that answered their question or not I'm not sure. I tried. After the speech, my gracious host, S.N. Rajan, and I joined the faculty for a late supper. I was interested that I kept meeting academics who had obtained or were working on doctorates in communications, not journalism per se. When they asked me which universities in the states were offering advanced graduate degrees in communications, I could only name a handful.

I also was asked if "big names" like TV's Barbara Walters, Tom Brokaw, or Dan Rather had Ph.Ds. I didn't think so. They seemed surprised. I understand that one needs graduate degrees to advance in academia, but it surprised me that so few had practical experience in journalism outside the classroom.

Finally, I met with Mrs. Zalina Abdul Halim, a young Muslim wife, mother and University of Malaysia law professor. We had become acquainted at the Bangkok conference. Zalina, a well-educated, attractive woman, who wore a traditional long, flowing gray silk dress and a head covering to match, worried about her weight like women everywhere.

She wanted to buy one of actress Jane Fonda's workout tapes so she and her sister-in-law could exercise.

So Zalina and I did what women do all over the world we had dinner and went shopping at a local mall in Kuala Lumpur.

At the Cu Chi Tunnels of Saigon
in July 2000 with a Vietnamese guide.

12

VIETNAM & CAMBODIA
30 Years Later

My return to Vietnam on July 4, 2000, U.S. Independence Day, was bittersweet and left me more depressed than I thought it would. I was filled with memories of friends and colleagues from the 1970s—all of us young and proud that we had been chosen by our respective news organizations to fill positions as reporters, writers, editors, and photographers in that difficult, distant place—but 30 years had taken its toll. Many of my pals died in bed, not on the battlefield. Or we simply lost touch.

How I wished I was with those friends once again, to walk down Tu Do Street, the main shopping thoroughfare in Saigon (now Ho Chi Minh City).

We could laugh and be curious together, noting that the old communications building where the infamous "Five O'clock Follies" military press conferences were held is now an upscale jewelry store. "The Follies" were the daily media briefings held at the appointed hour during the war which largely became a joke because of the discrepancies in how the media reported the war and the way the military and U.S. Embassy saw it. During those years, the media had access to fire fights, rocket attacks, and support bases which made military dissembling difficult to maintain.

There were other physical changes, too. The Hyatt Hotels gutted The Brinks (the Australian Army bachelor officers' quarters) to transform it into a luxury hotel. Burt Okuley and I emerged from dinner at The Brinks one night in 1971 to see a military guard fatally shoot a Vietnamese riding by on a motorcycle because, as the U.S. soldier said, he looked suspicious.

There was a leather briefcase attached to the rear of the cycle. When the briefcase was opened, there was only a raincoat and the man's lunch inside. The soldier was regretful, but it was too late.

There were renovations at other city landmarks, too, like the Continental Palace, Caravelle, and Majestic Hotels where we used to stand on the roofs to watch the fire fights across the Saigon River. Viet Cong guerrillas held forth on the other side of the river and no Americans dared go there. Now the skyline held towering neon signs—Hitachi, Fuji, Samsung—casting their glow upon the water.

I ate at a breakfast buffet in my hotel's rooftop café, then took a *cyclo* ride powered by an old man with outsized, gnarled legs from a lifetime of exercise. A *cyclo* in Southeast Asia is a three-wheeled pedaled or motorized taxi similar to a Chinese rickshaw. Later, I had a sundae at Ben & Jerry's in my hotel. The Communists may be in charge, but they certainly understand the merits of capitalism.

I had chosen to return to Vietnam one more time in 2000 when I was on the four-month journalism teaching fellowship in Asia. I had a poignant time by myself taking a trip down memory lane. Not only was I interested to visit old haunts, but I felt it was important to see what gains these besieged people had made in reuniting their country under a Communist regime.

In the early part of the last century, Saigon was known as the "Paris of the Far East." My cousin, Albert V. Dix (the Ohio publisher) spent many happy weeks there in the 1950s writing about

Indochina. Saigon could again be a tourist Mecca, but French-oriented Hanoi is a more likely prospect with its good restaurants, tree-lined streets, and bountiful shops.

I searched in vain for the restaurant Le Castelle on Tu Do Street, a short two block walk from the UPI bureau on Ngo Duc Ke Street and our main hangout, but it was replaced by a mini-mall.

Cheap Charlie's Chinese restaurant also was missing along with the Melody Bar, next to the bureau, and the Xinh Xinh (cute, cute) Bunny where the rats appeared at the bar along with the 11 p.m. curfew during the war. The Bunny owner used to say that the water he served was safe to drink, but we were skeptical of that claim when he dragged large blocks of ice across the street through the garbage and mud every morning.

As I searched for Le Castelle, I was reminded of the French owner who had a large, black Labrador who liked to greet diners while cadging food. One week in 1971, the owner complained to us that his food shipment for the week had disappeared coming down from the north on the Ho Chi Minh Trail. If he had no food to cook, he would have to close temporarily. We commiserated with him, and the Lab wagged its tail.

The next night, there were steaks and steak tartar on the menu, but the dog was never seen again. The owner only smiled. We always wondered.

I stopped by my old apartment house, The Kim Do, and strolled through the lobby. It was even tackier than I remembered it. The lobby was now decorated in cheap plastic chairs and ultra-feminine pink and white tulle and fake lace on the tables and windows. However, the old French lift was replaced by a single modern elevator. A restaurant was still located at the back of the building. I could have asked to see my old room with the kitchenette and the bathroom, but I didn't care.

One Sunday morning, my guide, a driver, and I drove 18 miles from Saigon to tour the Cu Chi Tunnels. During the war, it was widely rumored (but never proven) that the Vietnamese had built a network of underground tunnels where they could live and work during U.S. bombing raids. They are small people, but it seemed unbelievable. However, as the rumors grew, it was said that the tunnels extended from Saigon in the south to Hanoi in the north forming a long, underground, small city.

In reality, there apparently were four sets of tunnels scattered around the country, used as bomb shelters and containing medical facilities, kitchen, living and sleeping space. Generators cooled the tunnels; water and toilet facilities were built underground.

My guide recalled as a child visiting an aunt in Cu Chi during a bombing raid. "We spent six hours underground," she said, "and when we came up for air, my mother said, 'That's it. We won't be back until after the war.' It was a very unpleasant experience."

Bob Kaylor recalled taking a picture of a U.S. "tunnel rat" (a small American serviceman) crawling out of one of the tunnels in 1967 or 1968. He said the full extent of the tunnels was never discovered, although the present Cu Chi complex apparently was dug especially to show tourists. Certainly the adjoining gift shop wasn't part of the war.

I also visited Independence Palace, which was open to the public. The palace is furnished and looks much as it did when the late President Nguyen Van Thieu lived there. I even recognized the brown, overstuffed chair with lace doilies on the headrest and arms where I sat in 1970 in the family quarters to interview Madame Thieu. She said she prayed for peace every day.

In the basement of the palace, located in central Saigon, I entered Thieu's former office with the old maps of the war zones (I Corps, II Corps, etc.) still on the walls and held in place by thumbtacks. The old UPI and AP teletype machines were in the corner, silent for more than 25 years with the advent of computers. No wonder we lost the war with such obsolete communication facilities.

The American Embassy was leveled and there were plans to build a museum on the site.

Finally, I walked the few blocks to the old UPI bureau which is now a French-Vietnamese restaurant named after its address—Restaurant 19 in English. The four-story building was taller than I remembered it, the sandbags in front of the glass windows to deflect the rattling of gunfire were long gone, but the building still needed a paint job.

The owner's wife, who greeted me, was gracious and very accustomed to having UPI alums drop by. She offered me a glass of wine and a table covered with a white linen cloth and silverware. I chose a table where my old desk used to be in 1970, where I would throw a hairspray can at the roaches and other bugs crawling under the desk.

Her English was passable and we took a tour of the upper floor where we moved the second year I was there for some vague reason. That floor was now used for banquets and, "Where the Rotary Club meets on Tuesday," she said.

I opened the large closet door where the fellows from UPI audio, Jim Russell and Paul Vogel, broadcast their periodic radio reports by shortwave radio back to the United States. The airless closet used to be crammed with equipment and broadcast paraphernalia. Now it was used to store extra restaurant chairs. The single hanging light fixture was still in place.

I wanted to climb to the Cooks' former apartment at the top of the building and to see the old dormitory used by the combat reporters, but she didn't offer it and I was reluctant to impose on her hospitality.

Even with the rise of a new generation, the tour guides made sure that I didn't miss the relics of war in the guise of tourist attractions. When I flew to Hanoi, they made sure that I saw Ho Chi Minh's former home and museum. We also toured the previously-mentioned Hanoi Hilton where photos of former POW Naval aviator and now Senator John McCain were prominently displayed on the walls. There was a small plaque on a cell indicating where he had been incarcerated and his name. Half of the building is now a hotel with the other half retained as a prison museum. We crossed the Red River bridge–bombed frequently by U.S. planes—which has been rebuilt.

One of my favorite memories from the trip to North Vietnam was driving past a rice paddy en route to beautiful Ha Long Bay, a three-hour drive from Hanoi, past a barefoot Vietnamese farmer plodding along behind his water buffalo and hand plow, wearing a Walkman and swinging a bamboo baton in time to music only he could hear.

My guide and I boarded a fishing boat to tour Ha Long manned by three Vietnamese men and one of their wives. I was the only tourist. They provided a picnic lunch as we motored along looking at the giant rock formations in the bay and enjoying the scenery. Ha Long Bay has been designated a United Nations international historical site for its beauty.

I brought my bathing suit and went to the galley to change my clothes. I dove in to the warm water and paddled around for a few minutes while the group on deck watched me, jabbering in Vietnamese. I speak a little French, but only a few words of Vietnamese.

As I decided to return to the boat, I realized they were pointing and giggling. There was no ladder, no steps, and the deck was about three feet from the water line in calm, deep water. How was I going to get back on the boat?

Understand, I am a big western woman. I probably outweighed the three crewmen by 25 pounds. The guide suggested that they all jump overboard and push me up to the deck, but they couldn't swim. After much discussion, the guide said they would tow me to the shore, about a half mile away. I have my pride. I wasn't going to admit that I couldn't hoist myself up to the deck unaided.

I paddled around to the stern where a large metal drain pipe hung into the water. I pulled on it a few times and it seemed stable. So, like the nursery rhyme "Itsy-Bitsy Spider" that went up the water spout, I managed to pull myself up to the railing via the drain pipe and all hands on deck. By then, we were all laughing and joking in both languages about the crazy American woman who simply wanted to swim in the South China Sea. To celebrate my return, the captain brought out a bottle of rice wine and we drank our way back to shore.

Vietnam has made great strides in recovery, especially in the last two decades. Publications were proliferating in Hanoi and Saigon, although the government owns and operates the major ones. The advertising revenue reverts to the government coffers. The few English-language newspapers were filled with news from the government information ministry.

However, I was able to buy the *International Herald-Tribune* and *USA Today* in Hanoi and Saigon.

My colleague, Joe Ma Carlos—then of the Asian Media Information and Communication Center in Singapore—said he attempted to conduct a journalism workshop in Vietnam. He found the young reporters willing and anxious to learn, but really only familiar with government handouts or press releases. The fact that the government even let Carlos and other journalists talk to the reporters was significant in itself.

During the war, the English-language *Vietnam Guardian*, owned by a French-Vietnamese, used to pride itself on carrying titillating police stories of rape and incest on the front page. They would invariably note that it was necessary for the defendant male to have sex to "relieve his pressure." After reading a few of these stories every day, the reader began to believe that every man in Saigon must be severely repressed, certainly not evident in the spiraling birth rate. If the government objected to a story, a full page would run blank—which would only feed speculation, not stop it.

On his return to Vietnam during the 30th anniversary of the war's end, David Lamb of the *Los Angeles Times* noted that this country of 83 million people, has political stability now, a 94 percent literacy rate, a young, industrious population and a reliable work force. In 1990, the *Times* noted, nearly 51 percent of the population lived on less than one dollar a day. In 2004, the figure had shrunk to 10.6 percent.

On the downside, Lamb noted, the bureaucracy is thick and the pace of economic reform slow for foreign businesses. Vietnam's human rights record has improved, but falls short of international standards. Education remains poor in rural areas where 80 percent of the people live, and corruption remains an insurmountable problem.

The Communists evidently learned from their mistakes in Europe's eastern bloc countries where they suppressed religion, because the Buddhists, Catholics, and others practice religion openly. The Catholic Cathedral in Saigon was filled on Sunday mornings with parishioners, young and old.

There are more than 6,000 state-owned enterprises with some 1,000 privatized since 1993. The reeducation camps are a thing of the past. The country's major exports are clothing, shoes, crude petroleum, and seafood. Thailand and Vietnam are the world's leading rice exporters depending on the year and crop conditions.

Even with the rise of a new generation and increased prosperity, I came away with the impression that the Vietnamese don't care what kind of government they are living under, they are just happy to have peace and be left alone without outsiders telling them what to do. The Communists still refer to it as "America's war."

I don't expect to return to Vietnam, but I left with a good feeling about the country and its people. They are tough and tenacious and they will survive. They always have.

CAMBODIA

Neighboring Cambodia has a longer way to go—and they are a sad people—but they are trying hard to recover. They lost two million people in the war and to the atrocities of the Khmer Rouge and the Vietnamese. The streets are crowded in Phnom Penh with people who have lost limbs ostensibly from land mines.

After Vietnam, I spent a few days in Cambodia visiting the marvelous temples at Angkor Wat, which was closed to westerners during the fighting. The temples, dating to the 7th century, cover an area of 77 square miles in northwestern Cambodia. Many of the sites within this area have collapsed and only traces remain, and the grounds around others have not been cleared of land mines, but it is well worth the visit to see the temples that remain.

I also visited several rehabilitation/work centers funded by the Cambodian government and UNESCO (United Nations Economic, Social and Cultural Organization) where the disabled were taught to make beautiful native handicrafts and clothing. The workers were relentlessly cheerful even with their handicaps. Of course I felt the need to buy their wares.

A typical story of tragedy was described to me over dinner by my English-speaking guide, Chan Sophea, of the Cambodian tourism ministry.

Sophea was 17 when she married a young college professor at her home in southern Cambodia. The family was middle-class, her father a prosperous businessman. They owned their own home. The young couple had two children. One day, the Khmer Rouge knocked on the door. When her father answered, they fatally shot him in the head, then systematically executed the mother, Sophea's husband, and the two children. I asked her why she thought she was spared.

"I have the ability to sew," she said, "and I had repaired and made uniforms for the Khmer Rouge. I guess that I was of value to them, so they spared my life."

Sophea said that she cried every day for three years as she thought of the family that she lost. Then, when the Khmer Rouge and the Pol Pot government were driven out, she sold the family home to a neighbor, moved to Phnom Penh, and eventually was hired by the tourism ministry because of her ability to speak English.

She remarried, to a co-worker, and they have two children.

It was interesting to me in both Vietnam and Cambodia that the national monuments generally were spared damage during the fighting. The Angkor Wat temples at Siem Reap essentially were left intact—so was the national palace and museum in Phnom Penh and the beautiful Vinh Trang pagoda in My Tho, Vietnam. Angkor Wat was designated a U.N. world heritage site. As an Asian remarked: "They killed people, not monuments."

But as Sophea said to me, "Life must go on, even if it seems impossible at times."

At a Hong Kong party in 2000.

13

ETHIOPIA
Content Matters

Show me a country that has been occupied down through history by the Italians, Greeks, or French and I'll show you a country with decent restaurants and good food.

Granted, this is only my theory, but I found it to be true in Vietnam where the French controlled Indochina for more than 100 years, in Ethiopia where the Italians were the occupiers, and in little Albania where there is a pizza parlor or a Greek café on nearly every downtown corner. They may be poor countries, but the food is well-prepared, cheap, and plentiful except in the years of crop failure.

These countries have their native foods, too, but the invaders or neighboring countries taught them the art of cooking. Ethiopian culture was influenced by Egypt and Greece, but this ancient country of Emperor Haile Selassie "The Lion of Judah" was invaded by Italy in 1880 and again in 1936. British forces freed Ethiopia in 1941.

Albania is bordered by Greece on the south and Italy/Sicily lie across the Adriatic Sea. Italy invaded Albania at the start of World War II. Later, the Communists took over followed by the tyranny of Enver Hoxha who oppressed his people for four decades in a closed society. Dotting the beautiful countryside are the infamous cement bunkers (that look like giant mushrooms) which Hoxha said were needed to repel "invaders."

After I returned from the Knight Fellowship in Asia, I applied and received two teaching trips under the U.S. State Department's Office of International Information Programs. I taught journalism workshops in Ethiopia and Albania. I also flew to Johannesburg, South Africa one month after 9/11 to speak at a journalism conference of African nations at the State Department's request.

Heading for Jo-burg, airport security confiscated a nail file from my purse at John F. Kennedy Airport in New York which made me angry at myself for not removing the file. I had visited the World Trade Center site before I left for the airport—I was shocked at the devastation as everyone was—and I should have known better than to carry a sharp instrument. I am not a neophyte traveler.

Ethiopia—which has seen famine, strife, and upheaval for centuries—is still a proud country trying to push forward into the 21st century. Albania, especially the capital city of Tirana, also is moving forward although it is the third poorest country in Europe behind Moldova and even Romania, which in recent months has received financial help from the movie industry as a site location. Albania and Ethiopia were under communist control and South Africa dealt with apartheid for many years. The problems were different, but the people suffered.

I arrived in the capital city of Addis Ababa, Ethiopia in late July 2001 for two weeks to teach journalism workshops. Young journalists in Ethiopia work under difficult conditions in this emerging democracy because even with limited constitutional safeguards, they are dealing with a government and bureaucracy with little understanding of freedom of access to information and little tolerance for the people's right to know.

Fear of being thrown in jail for what they write is a constant threat, but the journalists persevere under frustrating circumstances. As one reporter explained it: "I put in a call to a government agency to get a comment on their side of the story, but by the time they get back to me, days and weeks have passed and I have moved on to other stories or I forgot what I wanted from them. It may be intentional on the government's part, but it certainly hurts objectivity."

The five days of formal workshops were held at the Semien Hotel in Addis, a commercial hotel in center city with a microphone setup and a VCR. The journalists sat at tables facing the speakers. Complimentary lunch and coffee/tea breaks were provided by the U.S. Embassy to the attendees who ranged in experience from beginning reporters and editors to middle/senior management.

Early on, I suggested doing writing tests and role-playing, but the attendees were uncomfortable with that idea because of the language difficulties. There are over 200 languages or dialects spoken in Ethiopia, the prime language being Amharic.

There are more than 70 weekly and daily publications operating there, some privately-owned, some government-owned, some published in Amharic, but many in English. Radio stations proliferated across the country, but the government operates the only TV station.

The valued reporters there, as elsewhere, are those who can cover and write a story in Amharic and then translate into English or vice versa for their publications, all on deadline. Computers are used on a limited basis.

I was frustrated the first two days because I didn't see how I could help them become better reporters and editors given their understandable attitude that, "We can't do that here. The government wouldn't allow it."

Fresh in their minds was the outbreak of violence in April 2000 at the local university when riot police broke up a student strike calling for greater freedom of expression and the removal of campus police. At the end of three days of turmoil, there were 39 dead, over 250 injured and some of the protesters were still in jail when I arrived. It was considered to be the bloodiest bout of civil unrest in Addis Ababa in a decade.

On the third day of the workshop, the embassy asked attorney Seleshi Ketsela to speak on the fact that there were protections afforded to Ethiopian journalists under the Constitution even if the government of Prime Minister Meles Zenawi interpreted the legal code as they wished.

Ketsela, who spoke in Amharic and answered questions for more than two hours, was an independent lawyer in Addis who represented a number of detained independent journalists during the university uprising so they did have some legal recourse.

Strange incidents happened to me in this East African country, however. The hotel switchboard put calls through to my room on two or three occasions from strangers asking if I would carry money or a package to someone's relative in the United States. I of course said no, but it is not uncommon for young people traveling abroad to be asked to carry drugs or other illicit items out of a country. Long jail terms often follow and the embassies have little ability to help the carriers if they get caught.

On another occasion, I shopped in an art store down the street from the hotel. Two polite young men offered to carry my packages to the hotel gate where there was a security guard on duty. I tipped them for their help and entered the hotel. They weren't allowed past the gate.

However, then I started receiving late night phone calls

allegedly from these young men saying they needed rent money, that I seemed like a nice American, and could I give them money? No, I couldn't and wouldn't. I asked them how they got my room number and why had the switchboard called me?

I hesitated to tell the switchboard to hold my calls because my hosts at the embassy might be trying to reach me, but as a woman alone in a strange country, it unnerved me. The embassy interceded with the hotel on my behalf and the calls finally stopped. I think the young men either paid the security guard or the switchboard operator to locate my room, or maybe it was all a scam to prey on westerners.

One of my other learning experiences in Ethiopia was visiting the wonderful National Museum in Addis Ababa to see the skull and about 10 bones of "Lucy" (or Dinquinesh "thou art wonderful" to Ethiopians), among the world's oldest skeletons of a woman. Discovered in 1974, Lucy was believed to have lived in Hadar in rugged eastern Ethiopia about 3.5 million years ago. I met a woman archaeologist who was on the original excavation team. A westerner, she confirmed that Lucy was named for the John Lennon/Paul McCartney song *Lucy in the Sky With Diamonds* which was playing on a tape recorder in camp the day that the bones were discovered.

I had a revealing conversation with a group of educated Ethiopian women at an embassy gathering one night when one of the women said, "We think American women work as hard or harder than women anywhere. Most of your women work outside the home, have children, husbands, large homes and do volunteer work. We do some of that, too, but we have servants and nannies to help us with the cleaning, the cooking, and child care. Labor is cheap and plentiful here. We are really in awe of how much American women do without help. It is tiring to think about." I thanked her for her concern.

During the second week of my visit, I joined a group from the embassy information staff for a tour to Southern Ethiopia on the only north/south paved road in the country. We traveled through the Great Rift Valley which looked like scenes from the Discovery Channel with miles and miles of scattered flattop, feathery trees and few inhabitants.

Along the way, we made village stops at offices of the Ethiopian News Agency (one computer and a female operator) and a couple of other news agencies.

We overnighted in the small city of Awasa on Lake Awasa, near the Kenyan border. Like many towns in the area, there are too many people—too few wearing shoes—living in thatched huts without electricity, covering themselves with giant banana fronds in lieu of raincoats to keep out the cold and rain, growing sweet corn and potatoes as they have for generations despite fertile soil which could be cultivated. Coffee is their chief export crop.

The countryside is a long way from Addis Ababa in terms of development.

And yet, Ethiopians are a good-looking, friendly people with a rich history dating back to Biblical times. They have been through a lot and they have suffered much, but they carry on.

My friend Helen Thomas jokes that half the cab drivers in Washington, D. C., are from Ethiopia, and indeed it seems that way.

We returned to Addis to visit a newspaper called *Fortune*, an independent business weekly that seems to be thriving in an old villa with a large staff. The slogan on the masthead says "Content Matters." My guide and translator, Tabotu T. Woldemichael from the embassy staff, and I spent time with *Fortune* managing editor Tamrat G. Giorgis, an engaging fellow who gained his experience working on the Akron, Ohio, *Beacon Journal* on a fellowship program. He returned to Ethiopia to start his own paper, a good one.

When I told him I was born near Akron, he said, "Well, you'll have to admit that Addis is more fun than Akron." He was right.

Since the State Department only permits its employees and contract workers to fly tourist class, I flew nine hours from Addis Ababa to Rome, a tiring trip. I got to my hotel room in Rome and looked at my watch. It was only 8 p.m. In wonderful Rome. On a Saturday night. I couldn't go to bed and miss out on all the city has to offer. I went to the hotel lobby, hailed a cab, and went to the Spanish Steps to mix with the evening throng of tourists and Italians. I had dinner at McDonald's up the street. Love that city.

In October 2002, I visited the Republic of Albania, again to teach. With a population of 3.5 million people and 40% unemployment, the country must clean up corruption and their reputation as a center for trafficking drugs and women before they can be considered serious candidates for membership in the European Union and NATO. However, the Bush administration listed them among the countries who supported the U.S. invasion of Iraq and there is a sizeable Albanian population in America. Albania is a Muslim, Albanian Orthodox, and Roman Catholic country.

The business journalists, most of whom work for publications representing political and religious factions in the country, watch CNN and BBC, so they were well aware of Enron and other corporate scandals. There is compulsory, free education in Albania and most of the reporters/editors at their journalism center had some university background.

Foreign investment is minimal, which keeps the country from progressing, but until corruption is resolved things are unlikely to change. Embassy figures showed that Coca-Cola was the largest American investor. The Danes and other Scandinavian countries also have contributed to the economy. Tourism could be developed there because they have many ancient ruins, but it takes leadership.

Mayor Edi Rama, a former artist, is attempting to cover the "Communist gray" of the numerous government buildings by painting them bright pastels to improve the city's image, but many of the hotels stand empty for lack of tourists.

After my Albanian trip, the State Department put the international information and teaching programs on hold. That caused conflicting opinions among many of us. The capable head of the program, Ellen Toomey, retired to Maine; the war in Iraq dragged on; and American journalism was hit with a series of internal scandals that caused great angst and bad publicity within the industry.

To the credit of major newspapers like *The New York Times* and *USA Today*, they moved quickly to remove the miscreants, but I have often thought: how can I go overseas to emerging democracies to tell them how to cover their news ethically, honestly, and fairly when we have been guilty of so many missteps here? For a while, it became like the old bromide "don't do as we do, do as we say."

It was a sad, embarrassing period for reporters, editors, photographers and publishers who have made journalism a way of life. We are proud of what we do and with good reason. And if you'll permit me one more cliche, we don't need a few bad apples to spoil it for the rest of us.

In front of the National
Assembly Building in Saigon
with the troops, 1970.

14

Mexico, Munich & More: Traveling the Globe

I t is apparent from what I have written up to this point that I love to travel. The phone rings, an invitation comes, and I'm out the door. Blame it again on my restless nature.

The need for increased security at airports and other transportation points has taken the luster off getting from Point A to Point B, but I'm not ready to sit home and look at four walls when there are new places to explore and interesting people to meet. Fortunately, my friends and I have had jobs that included travel at someone else's expense, which has eased the financial burden.

One of my earliest trips after I started working in New Jersey was to Mexico with a small tour group that included a very charming Latino guide. If I am on a tour alone, I always make friends with the tour guides because they will take me to sites after-hours that I might not see with a group.

This can become a bore, as it was in Hanoi, when the tour guide joined me at every meal and, of course, let me pay the dinner bills, but he was knowledgeable about North Vietnam and I learned from him. He also was part of the group who couldn't figure out how to get me back aboard ship at Ha Long Bay when I went swimming without a boat ladder in the South China Sea.

But I digress. The Mexican guide and I were dining at a hotel in

Acapulco one night under a full moon with the soft breezes blowing. It was a romantic setting and being a Latino macho man he started giving me compliments on my hair, my dress, and my personality. I led him on for a while and then I laughingly said, "Jose, you lie. You don't mean a word of what you are saying."

Then, he laughed, too. "*Si senora...but eet ees the custom.*" At least he didn't expect a big tip for his line.

My first trip to Europe, before the press club's eastern bloc trip, came when I bummed around several countries on the cheap, carrying several books telling me how to travel on $5 or $10 a day, and being able to do so by staying in *pensiones* and eating in cafeterias.

I never quite subscribed to the theory that if you stay with the natives, you learn more about their country and how they live. That's difficult to do when you don't speak their language and you are merely a tenant on their property. Besides, if you run a *pensione* or a hotel, you stay home or at the reservation desk and watch television. What fun is that?

I was awakened at an Italian pensione one night—with my wallet and my passport hidden under my pillow—and watched in the moonlight while the door knob on my room door was silently turned. I rolled over on the creaking bed springs and it stopped. I got up and moved a chair in front of the door and went back to sleep. I wonder what he or she wanted?

I had always planned to see Berlin—still a divided city, but rebuilt in the western sector from the devastation of World War II. I'm not sure that it was dangerous to be there, but I perceived that it was, so I listed myself on the visa application as a schoolteacher, not a journalist, to avoid questions. The Wall dividing the city was a sobering experience, to see the bleak, unpainted buildings at the border crossing when Communist guards checked our bus carefully, running mirrors on the underside looking for explosives or escaping stowaways, although it seemed unlikely that people would want to escape to the East except to see relatives.

In an historic step, the Berlin Wall was opened in November 1989 after a plea by President Ronald Reagan to the Russians to "take down this wall."

I saw my first strip show in Berlin, a raucous event where the crowd clapped and whistled at the scantily-clad men and women performing simulated sex with a variety of animals on stage. The animals looked bewildered.

Aside from the nightlife, Berlin is a very sophisticated city of parks and monuments that must have been wonderful before Hitler's rise to prominence and the war. The author Christopher Isherwood wrote movingly of Berlin in the '30s in his autobiographical collection *Berlin Stories,* which later was made into the popular musical *Cabaret* and the play *I Am a Camera.*

I later visited the Nazi concentration camp at Dachau which brought the horror of that historical period into focus. I joined my longtime family friend Don Thompson and his German friends, Hermann and Hanna Schwarze, for a trip to mountainous southern Bavaria with a stop at Oktoberfest in Munich to drink huge steins of beer, eat finger-lickin' good chicken, and link arms with our companions at long tables covered with white paper tablecloths to sing German and American songs into the night.

We still greet each other by breaking into Frank Sinatra's "Strangers in Zee Night," "Two Hearts Togezzer" as we sang it with the German accent. Don and I also made the crossing together on the QEII when I came home from Vietnam.

It was a helpful experience to travel with German-speaking residents of this now prosperous country and to meet gracious people, once our enemy, on their turf. Hermann and Hanna were part of the post-war generation.

One of the highlights of that trip was the stop in the medieval town of Rothenburg, one of the three great walled cities of Germany and a popular tourist attraction. Wherever I have lived, from Vietnam to California, I have hung little pictures of that town by my front door as a good luck charm because I enjoyed it so much.

With more than 1,000 years of history behind it, there is a legend about the scenic little town which dates back to 1631 when the 30 Years War was raging between the Catholics and Protestants. Rothenburg, a Protestant town, was about to be overrun by a Catholic army.

Just before the battle was to begin, the Catholic general offered a deal. If anyone could drink a three-liter tankard of wine in one gulp, the town would be spared. Rothenburg's mayor, named Nusch, rushed forward to take the challenge. He grabbed the tankard, swilled down the wine in one gulp, and passed out for three days. The town rejoiced over his extraordinary commitment to civic duty.

His feat is immortalized in the clock on the Councilors' Tavern in the marketplace. At certain hours of the day, the clock's large wooden figures reenact the mayor's sacrificial gulp for his people while a Catholic general urges him on.

It is also said that the town was spared damage during World War II when a German general appealed to the U.S. military and its allies to avoid bombing the area because of its historical value.

In other villages, we saw the cows coming down from summer pasture adorned with flowered straw hats. One or two other cows wore elaborate crosses as head dresses. When Hanna asked a shepherd the significance of the cross decoration, she was told that each cross was in memory of an animal that had fallen off the edge of a mountain cliff and died.

I left Don and the Schwarzes in Munich and boarded a train for Rome, nursing the granddaddy of all colds. I was in a compartment on the train with a man about my age, an Italian. As the train rumbled along, I stood up with my back to him and suddenly, as many Italian men are wont to do, he pinched my bottom. I swung around and suddenly let out a giant sneeze, which hit him in the face. I apologized, but he just stared, got up, and left the compartment, never to be seen again. I felt so miserable that I got off the train in Verona, found a nearby pensione, and went to bed for three days to recover.

In 1987, my sister Martha and I took her two oldest children, Jason and Courtney, to France and Italy for an educational excursion. Being young teenagers, they were more enchanted with the air-conditioned McDonald's franchises than the fancy French restaurants, but we had a good time and saw a lot.

Jason, a tall, handsome young man, always said that I brought him along to carry my as-usual-overpacked luggage. I taught him to drink martinis on that trip and we managed to clear out the mini-bar in our Paris hotel drinking Chartreuse.

The children liked to tell about the night I got into a fight with the gondola driver in Venice when he refused to take us on a late night canal trip. I wanted them to have the experience of a gondola ride, but he was having none of two women and two teenagers. I speak limited Italian, but I didn't grow up in Westfield with Italian immigrants for nothing. Somehow the situation deteriorated. I was cursing and exchanging rude gestures with the gondolier, which only the Italians can do with style.

My sister was afraid the *carabinieri* (Italian police) would arrive to quell the disturbance. The gondolier solved the impasse by simply paddling away. I lost the battle and I lost the war, but I didn't care. One of the last conversations Jason and I had before he died was to reminisce about the gondola incident and the laughs we had on the European trip.

As he noted: Don't mess with Aunt Maggie when she wants to do something. She doesn't take no for an answer.

Mother and I traveled together a lot after she was widowed, including the eastern bloc trip with the press club. She never quite forgave me for refusing to let her visit Vietnam when she was on a trip to Japan and Taiwan with a friend while I was still in Saigon. I had no excuse except that I was working and I didn't want to entertain guests—street crime was rampant there and I was concerned that they would be robbed—and I just didn't want to have to be worried about two elderly women in a war zone. It was a selfish attitude, no doubt, but I chose to meet her in Tokyo instead.

We also took an 11-day cruise up the Nile in Egypt from Cairo to the ancient tombs, to Luxor and Aswan Dam. We climbed into King Tut's tomb and saw the sound and light show at the Pyramids at nightfall. Mother liked to joke that she taught the Muslim waiters on the ship to make a decent martini, adding vermouth instead of water. We wearied of eating lamb, their meat of choice.

Mother and I had a tacit agreement on our trips that if either of us met an interesting man, the other would fade into the woodwork to let the relationship proceed. This worked better for me than it did for her. She complained at breakfast one morning that a charming gentleman she met on the ship the night before spent the entire evening talking about his ailments.

"I guess I have to expect that at my age," she opined, "but here we are in this fascinating country on this nice ship and all he could talk about were his prostate problems. I mean, really!"

A crew member, a polite young Egyptian man who spoke fluent English, took to visiting me late in the evening to talk politics, standing on the deck outside our cabin and conversing through the open window. He said that he knew I was a journalist because he had overheard a dinner conversation. I never did see his face clearly in the dark, but he seemed sincere in wanting peace for that troubled part of the world.

Mother and I knew that it probably would be our last trip together because she had suffered several heart attacks, but we determined to make the most of our time together. She died on Christmas day 1983 while visiting us at Martha and Norm's home in Stockton. I always will be glad that we were close and able to take good trips together.

And I hope that I have many years of travel ahead of me. I still want to return to Africa and go on safari. I also would like to visit South America and spend more time in the British Isles perhaps visiting our ancestral locale in Ireland, if I can find it.

And I would say to you in closing: wherever you go, whatever you do, remember to laugh.

It helps.

INDEX

U

Uebberoth, Peter 142
Ulrey, Lewis V. 26-28, 37
U.S.S. Constellation 109

V

Van Buren, Abigail 145
Van Thieu, Nguyen 86, 92, 106, 168
Venice 191
Vietnam 13, 18, 45, 68, 85-98, 102-111, 115, 148, 151, 165-174, 177, 187, 189, 190
Vietnam War 97

W

Walters, Barbara 128, 162
Watergate 116
Westfield, NY 37-48, 141, 191
Williams, Harrison A. 60
Women's National Press Club 28, 78, 82, 85, 114
Wooster, OH 24, 25, 28, 29, 36-38, 47, 48

About the Author

During more than four decades in journalism, Margaret (Maggie) A. Kilgore worked 16 years for United Press International in Ohio, New Jersey and Washington, D.C. where she covered Congress, the White House and the Justice Department. She is a past president of the former Women's National Press Club in Washington. She was a foreign correspondent for the wire service during the Vietnam War from 1970-72.

In 1973, Kilgore joined the *Los Angeles Times* as a financial and general assignment reporter. She later worked for a decade in corporate public relations. She was the recipient of a Ford Foundation Walter Lippmann Fellowship and Knight International Press Fellowship. She also has conducted economic journalism workshops in emerging democracies for the U.S. State Department in Asia, Africa and Europe. Miss Kilgore lives in Santa Monica, CA.

www.maggiekilgore.com

We're Still Here: Contemporary Virginia Indians Tell Their Stories

Sandra Wauagaman & Danielle Moretti-Langholtz, Ph.D.
ISBN 1928662013, $14.95, paperback

Just updated for 2006 to include:
- Jamestown 2007
- Werowocomoco
- National Museum of the American Indian
- Teacher's resource guide

"This book fills a void...It covers all of the tribes, and is informative, but easy to read."

--Joyce Krigsvold, Paumunkey Indian Museum

The 7 Most Powerful Selling Secrets

John Livesay
ISBN 1928662048, $19.95, hardcover

""John Livesay's book identifies three critical ingredients to mastering the 'art of salesmanship' for today's business world - your voice, your energy, and your soul. John's unique insights into humanizing the sales experience makes this book a "must-read" for newcomers, as well as seasoned vets. If you are looking for opportunities to update your tools of the trade and gain a competitive advantage in the sales arena, then look no further than this book!"
--Kevin Carroll, Creative Motivator to Nike designers (aka The Katalyst), Nike

---

Poor Man's Philanthropist: The Thomas Cannon Story

Sandra Waugaman with Thomas *Cannon*
ISBN 1928662056, $23.95, hardcover

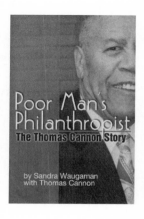

Thomas Cannon (referred to as "The Poor Man's Philanthropist) was a retired postal worker of modest means who awarded gifts of $1,000 to deserving individuals. Over the past three decades, Cannon, a retired postal worker, had given $146,000, usually in $1,000 checks, to individuals he felt were setting an example for others. Read about his inspiring life story.

"Cannon is now a legend in Richmond."
-- Parade Magazine

200

BUY DIRECT FROM PALARI

Save with free shipping on these titles.

Remember to Laugh

Writing My Way Around the World

Maggie Kilgore
(ISBN 1928662374)
$22.00, hardcover

Remember FREE SHIPPING when ordered with this form!

Deliver books to:

Name_____

Phone_____-_____Email_____

Address_____

City_____State_____Zip_____

		Number of Books	Total
We're Still Here	$14.95 X	_____	=_____
The 7 Selling Secrets	$19.95 X	_____	=_____
Poor Man's Philanthropist	$23.95 X	_____	=_____
Remember to Laugh	$22.00 X	_____	=_____

VA residents add 5.0% sales tax = _____

TOTAL ENCLOSED = _____

Order online at WWW.PALARIBOOKS.com
or send check or money order to
Palari Publishing
P. O. Box 9288
Richmond, Virginia 23227-0288